easy pasta dinners

GRAND
AVENUE
BOOKS

Grand Avenue Books

An imprint of Meredith® Corporation

Easy Pasta Dinners

Contributing Editors: Sharyl Heiken, Rosemary Hutchinson
   (Spectrum Communication Services)

Contributing Designer: Joline Rivera

Copy and Production Editor: Victoria Forlini

Copy Chief: Terri Fredrickson

Contributing Proofreaders: Gretchen Kauffman, Susan J. Kling

Editorial Operations Manager: Karen Schirm

Manager, Book Production: Rick von Holdt

Editorial and Design Assistants: Karen McFadden, Mary Lee Gavin, Patricia Loder

Grand Avenue Books

Editor In Chief: Linda Raglan Cunningham

Design Director: Matt Strelecki

Executive Editor, Grand Avenue Books: Dan Rosenberg

Publisher: James D. Blume

Executive Director, Marketing: Jeffrey Myers

Executive Director, New Business Development: Todd M. Davis

Executive Director, Sales: Ken Zagor

Director, Operations: George A. Susral

Director, Production: Douglas M. Johnston

Business Director: Jim Leonard

Vice President and General Manager: Douglas J. Guendel

Meredith Publishing Group

President, Publishing Group: Stephen M. Lacy

Vice President-Publishing Director: Bob Mate

Meredith Corporation

Chairman and Chief Executive Officer: William T. Kerr

In Memoriam: E.T. Meredith III (1933–2003)

All of us at Grand Avenue Books are dedicated to providing you with the information and ideas you need to create delicious foods. We welcome your comments and suggestions. Write to us at: Grand Avenue Books, Editorial Department LN-114, 1716 Locust Street, Des Moines, IA 50309-3023

Pictured on front cover: Lemon-Pepper Pasta and Chicken (see recipe, page 40)

Library of Congress Control Number: 2002111432

ISBN: 0-696-21686-8

AMAZING PASTA

When it comes to creating great-tasting meals, pasta is the busy cook's ace in the hole. This versatile ingredient comes in a myriad of shapes and sizes, cooks with a minimum of fuss, and can be either everyday or elegant depending on the sauce or other fixings you put with it. What's more, pasta works equally well for spur-of-the-moment or plan-ahead meals.

Now with the help of *Easy Pasta Dinners,* you can make the most of pasta for your meals. The more than 100 imaginative recipes range from captivating skillet specialties, saucepan meals, and toss-and-serve entrées to distinctive soups, main-dish salads, and side dishes. All of these innovative ideas are designed to please families, use ordinary ingredients, and go from cupboard or refrigerator to table in a flash— most in 30 minutes or less.

You can choose from meat, poultry, fish or seafood, and meatless main dishes. For family meals, make Southwest Beef-Linguine Toss, Pasta with Pepperoni Marinara, or Chicken and Pasta Toss. Or if you're looking for something a bit more adventuresome, try Roasted Red Pepper Sauce over Tortellini, Linguine with Fennel and Shrimp in Orange Sauce, or Lemon-Pepper Pasta and Chicken. When you're in the mood for soup or a salad, check out Asian Chicken Noodle Soup, Tuscan Ravioli Stew, Salmon-Pasta Salad, or Fontina and Melon Salad. And to round out meals, opt for sides such as Mixed Pastas with Fresh Herbs or Mexican-Style Spaghetti.

In addition to ideas for mouthwatering meals, *Easy Pasta Dinners* also provides you with quick-reference identification photos and handy cooking directions to help take the guesswork out of preparing pasta.

Take advantage of the lively recipes in *Easy Pasta Dinners* to enjoy pasta whenever and as often as you like. How about tonight?

Fettuccine and Salmon
(see recipe, page 98)

PASTA AT A GLANCE 6

Identifying and cooking different kinds of pasta is a cinch with this pasta primer.

SKILLET DISHES 10

These pasta main dishes will show you how sensational supper in a skillet can be.

SAUCEPAN FAVORITES 78

A saucepan is all it takes to simmer these tempting pasta entrées.

EASY OVEN DISHES 120

Tuck these no-fuss pastas in the oven and let them bake to perfection.

SOUPS 140

Ladle up comforting bowls of these chock-full-of-pasta pleasers tonight.

TOSS & SERVE ENTRÉES 164

Start with cooked pasta, toss in a few simple ingredients, and dinner is served.

MAIN-DISH SALADS 182

These hearty salads feature everything from elbow macaroni to orzo to tortellini.

SIDE DISHES 212

Skip the potatoes and round out your meal with one of these pasta medleys.

INDEX 250

PASTA AT A GLANCE

If the many shapes and sizes coupled with sometimes exotic names make pasta seem confusing, these helpful photos of 30 common shapes will help straighten things out.

Acini di Pepe: Tiny rounds resembling whole peppercorns that often are used in soups

Angel Hair (Capellini): Extremely fine strands the length of spaghetti

Nested Angel Hair (Capellini): Extremely fine strands rolled into coils

Bow Ties, large (Farfalle): Flat pieces pinched in the center to form bow-tie or butterfly shapes

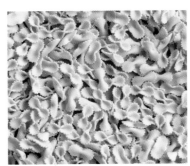

Bow Ties, tiny (Tripolini): Miniature bow ties or butterflies that often are used in soups

Cavatelli: Ridged elongated shells that have their edges curled inward

Corkscrew Macaroni (Rotini): Short twisted strands that can be loosely or tightly spiraled

Ditalini: Small tubes that resemble tiny thimble; often used in soups

Elbow Macaroni: Short tubes curved into half circles often used in casseroles and soups

Fettuccine: 1/4-inch ribbons about the length of spaghetti

Fusilli: Strands the length of spaghetti twisted into a corkscrew shape

Gemelli: Short strands that look like two pieces of rope twisted together

Lasagna: Large flat ribbons, some with ruffled edges, often used in casseroles

Linguine: 1/8-inch ribbons about the length of spaghetti

Mafalda: 3/4-inch ribbons with ruffled edges; about the length of spaghetti

Manicotti: Large hollow tubes, sometimes cut diagonally on the ends, designed to be filled

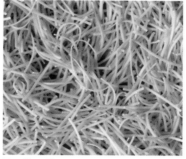

Noodles, fine: Pasta made with eggs or egg yolks, cut into thin, short strands

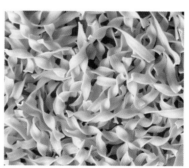

Noodles, medium: Pasta made with eggs or egg yolks and cut into 1/4-inch or wider strands

Orzo (Rosamarina): tiny pieces that resemble rice; often used in soups

Penne (Mostaccioli): Slender, smooth, or ridged tubes with ends cut diagonally

Ravioli: Stuffed pillows of pasta that can be square or round

Rigatoni: Ridged tubes that are about 2 inches long and ½ inch wide; often used in casseroles

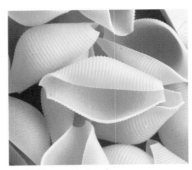

Shell Macaroni, jumbo (Conchiglioni): Conch-shaped shells designed to hold a filling

Shell Macaroni, tiny (Conchigliette): Tiny seashell shapes often used in soups

Spaghetti: Long rod-shaped strands

Tortellini: Circles of pasta folded over a filling and shaped into rings

Vermicelli: Thin strands similar in shape to spaghetti

Nested Vermicelli: Thin strands similar in shape to spaghetti that are rolled into coils

Wagon Wheel Macaroni (Ruote): Pasta that is shaped like the spokes of a wheel

Ziti: Tube-shaped strands the length of spaghetti or cut into shorter pieces

Mixing and Matching Pastas and Sauces: Sometimes deciding what type of pasta to serve with your favorite sauces is confusing. Here are a few hints to help you make the best choices. Match thin sauces with delicate pastas such as angel hair pasta, fettuccine, or vermicelli. Team chunky sauces with pastas that have holes or ridges. Corkscrew macaroni (rotini), rigatoni, and penne (mostaccioli) are all ideal. Pair heavy sauces with thicker pastas, such as fettuccine, ziti, or mafalda. Also, consider ease of eating when choosing a pasta. Long strands which will be wrapped around a fork are best with sauces that have small pieces. Sauces with bigger pieces are better suited to shorter pastas that can be scooped up with a fork. Smooth sauces work with any kind of pasta.

Cooking Packaged Pasta

Perfectly cooked pasta makes an ideal side dish for almost any menu. For just-right doneness, place 3 quarts of water for 4 to 8 ounces of pasta in a large saucepan. Bring the water to boiling. If you like, add 1 teaspoon salt and 1 tablespoon olive or cooking oil to help keep the pasta separate. Add the pasta, a little at a time, so the water does not stop boiling. (For long pasta, dip one end into the water. As the pasta softens, gently curl it around the pan and into the water.) Reduce the heat slightly. Boil, uncovered, for the time listed below or until the pasta is tender but slightly firm (al dente). (The timings listed are only guidelines. Be sure to check package directions because cooking times vary by brand.) Stir occasionally and test often for doneness. Drain.

Packaged Dried Pasta	Cooking Time
Acini de Pepe	5 to 6 minutes
Angel Hair (Capellini)	5 to 6 minutes
Bow Ties, large (Farfalle)	about 10 minutes
Bow Ties, tiny (Tripolini)	5 to 6 minutes
Cavatelli	about 12 minutes
Corkscrew Macaroni (Rotini)	8 to 10 minutes
Ditalini	7 to 9 minutes
Elbow Macaroni	about 10 minutes
Fettuccine	8 to 10 minutes
Fusilli	about 15 minutes
Gemelli	about 10 minutes
Lasagna	10 to 12 minutes
Linguine	8 to 10 minutes
Mafalda	10 to 12 minutes
Manicotti	about 18 minutes
Noodles	6 to 8 minutes
Orzo (Rosamarina)	5 to 8 minutes
Penne (Mostaccioli)	about 14 minutes
Rigatoni	about 15 minutes
Shell Macaroni, jumbo (Conchiglioni)	about 18 minutes
Shell Macaroni, tiny (Conchigliette)	8 to 9 minutes
Spaghetti	10 to 12 minutes
Tortellini	about 15 minutes
Vermicelli	5 to 7 minutes
Wagon Wheel Macaroni (Ruote)	about 15 minutes
Ziti	14 to 15 minutes

SKILLET DISHES

Whether stroganoff, primavera, or lo mein, these skillet favorites boast a world of wonderful flavor.

Hoisin-Glazed Turkey Medallions
(see recipe, page 51)

BAIL-OUT BEEF STROGANOFF

A hint of horseradish and fresh dill in the sour cream sauce enlivens this speedy version of the all-time favorite stroganoff.

Start to Finish: 30 minutes   **Makes:** 4 servings

3 cups dried wide noodles or mafalda (about 6 ounces)
3 cups broccoli spears
$1/2$ cup light dairy sour cream
$1^1/2$ teaspoons prepared horseradish
$1/2$ teaspoon snipped fresh dill
1 pound boneless beef ribeye steak, cut into thin bite-size strips

1 small onion, cut into $1/2$-inch slices
1 clove garlic, minced
1 tablespoon cooking oil
4 teaspoons all-purpose flour
$1/2$ teaspoon ground black pepper
1 14-ounce can beef broth
3 tablespoons tomato paste
1 teaspoon Worcestershire sauce

1

Cook noodles or pasta according to package directions, adding broccoli for the last 5 minutes of cooking. Drain. Cover and keep warm.

2

Meanwhile, in a small bowl stir together the sour cream, horseradish, and dill; cover and chill until serving time.

3

In a large skillet cook half of the beef, the onion, and garlic in hot oil until beef is done and onion is tender. Remove from skillet. Add remaining beef; cook and stir until beef is done. Return all meat to skillet; sprinkle flour and pepper over meat. Stir to coat.

4

Stir in broth, tomato paste, and Worcestershire sauce. Cook and stir until thickened and bubbly. Cook and stir for 1 minute more. Divide noodle-broccoli mixture among 4 bowls. Spoon beef mixture on top of noodle mixture. Serve with the horseradish-sour cream mixture.

Nutrition Facts per serving: 368 calories, 15 g total fat, 81 mg cholesterol, 454 mg sodium, 32 g carbohydrate, 29 g protein.

CHILI MACARONI

Round out the meal with a crisp green salad or fresh fruit.

Start to Finish: 25 minutes **Makes:** 4 servings

12 ounces lean ground beef or
   uncooked ground turkey
1 medium onion, chopped
1 14½-ounce can Mexican-style
   stewed tomatoes
1¼ cups tomato juice
2 tablespoons canned diced green
   chile peppers, drained
2 teaspoons chili powder

½ teaspoon garlic salt
1 cup dried wagon wheel macaroni
   (ruote) or elbow macaroni (about
   3 ounces)
1 cup loose-pack frozen cut green
   beans
1 cup shredded cheddar cheese
   (4 ounces)

1
In a large skillet cook the ground beef or turkey and onion until meat is browned. Drain off fat.

2
Stir stewed tomatoes, tomato juice, chile peppers, chili powder, and garlic salt into the meat mixture. Bring to boiling. Stir in uncooked pasta and green beans. Return to boiling; reduce heat. Cover and simmer about 15 minutes or until pasta and beans are tender.

3
To serve, spoon into bowls. Sprinkle with shredded cheddar cheese.

Nutrition Facts per serving: 427 calories, 21 g total fat, 83 mg cholesterol, 1,118 mg sodium, 32 g carbohydrate, 29 g protein.

TOMATOES AND RAVIOLI WITH ESCAROLE

For a change of pace, use cheese-filled ravioli or tortellini.

Start to Finish: 30 minutes **Makes:** 4 servings

1/2 cup chopped onion
2 cloves garlic, minced
1 tablespoon olive oil or cooking oil
3 cups sliced fresh mushrooms
2 cups chopped plum tomatoes
3/4 cup chicken broth
4 cups coarsely chopped escarole

1 tablespoon snipped fresh basil
1 teaspoon snipped fresh rosemary
1 9-ounce package refrigerated meat-filled ravioli or meat-filled tortellini
1/4 cup pine nuts, toasted

1

For sauce, in a large skillet cook onion and garlic in hot oil for 2 minutes. Add mushrooms, tomatoes, and chicken broth. Bring to boiling; reduce heat. Simmer, uncovered, about 7 minutes or until mushrooms are tender and sauce is slightly reduced (you should have about 3 cups sauce). Add escarole, basil, and rosemary, stirring just until the escarole is wilted.

2

Meanwhile, cook pasta according to package directions. Drain; return pasta to saucepan. Pour sauce over pasta; toss to coat. Transfer to a warm serving dish. Sprinkle with pine nuts.

Nutrition Facts per serving: 339 calories, 14 g total fat, 34 mg cholesterol, 454 mg sodium, 43 g carbohydrate, 16 g protein.

SOUTHWEST BEEF-LINGUINE TOSS

Bottled picante sauce contributes both flavor and sauciness.

Start to Finish: 25 minutes **Makes:** 4 servings

4 ounces dried linguine, fettuccine, or spaghetti
1 tablespoon cooking oil
2 teaspoons chili powder
1 clove garlic, minced
1 small onion, sliced and separated into rings
1 red or green sweet pepper, cut into strips

12 ounces beef top round steak, cut into thin bite-size strips
1 10-ounce package frozen whole kernel corn
$\frac{1}{4}$ cup bottled picante sauce
Fresh cilantro sprigs (optional)

1

Cook pasta according to package directions. Drain pasta; rinse with warm water. Drain again.

2

Meanwhile, heat oil in a wok or large skillet over medium-high heat. (Add more oil as necessary during cooking.) Stir-fry chili powder and garlic in hot oil for 15 seconds. Add onion; stir-fry for 1 minute. Add sweet pepper; stir-fry for 1 to 2 minutes more or until vegetables are crisp-tender. Remove vegetables from wok.

3

Add beef to wok. Stir-fry for 2 to 3 minutes or until done. Return vegetables to wok. Stir in corn and picante sauce. Add the cooked pasta. Toss to coat all ingredients. Cook and stir until heated through. If desired, garnish with cilantro.

Nutrition Facts per serving: 351 calories, 9 g total fat, 54 mg cholesterol, 166 mg sodium, 43 g carbohydrate, 27 g protein.

STIR-FRIED BEEF AND RAMEN NOODLES

Add extra Asian flair by using ¹/₄ teaspoon five-spice powder instead of the ground ginger.

Start to Finish: 30 minutes **Makes:** 3 servings

1 3-ounce package beef-flavored
   ramen noodles
1 tablespoon cooking oil
1 medium carrot, thinly sliced
1 stalk celery, bias sliced
8 ounces beef sirloin steak, cut into
   thin bite-size strips

1 6-ounce package frozen pea pods,
   thawed
¹/₄ cup water
1 tablespoon snipped fresh parsley
2 teaspoons bottled teriyaki sauce
¹/₂ teaspoon ground ginger
¹/₄ teaspoon crushed red pepper
   (optional)

1

Cook ramen noodles according to package directions, except drain the noodles and reserve the seasoning package.

2

Heat oil in a wok or large skillet over medium-high heat. (Add more oil as necessary during cooking.) Add carrot and celery. Stir-fry for 2 to 3 minutes or until crisp-tender. Remove vegetables from wok.

3

Add steak strips to hot wok. Stir-fry for 2 to 3 minutes or until done. Return carrot and celery to the wok. Stir in noodles, reserved seasoning package, pea pods, the water, parsley, teriyaki sauce, ginger, and, if desired, crushed red pepper. Cook over medium heat until heated through, stirring occasionally.

Nutrition Facts per serving: 621 calories, 30 g total fat, 50 mg cholesterol, 1,724 mg sodium, 61 g carbohydrate, 30 g protein.

BOW TIES WITH SAUSAGE AND SWEET PEPPERS

If you like, use Italian-style turkey sausage links to reduce the fat—but not the flavor.

Start to Finish: 25 minutes **Makes:** 4 servings

4 cups dried large bow ties (farfalle) or 3 cups dried medium shell macaroni (8 ounces)

12 ounces uncooked spicy Italian sausage links

2 medium red sweet peppers, cut into $^3/_4$-inch pieces

$^1/_2$ cup vegetable broth or beef broth

$^1/_4$ teaspoon coarsely ground black pepper

$^1/_4$ cup snipped fresh Italian parsley

1

Cook pasta according to package directions. Drain; return pasta to saucepan. Cover and keep warm.

2

Meanwhile, cut the sausage into 1-inch pieces. In a large skillet cook sausage and sweet peppers over medium-high heat until sausage is browned. Drain off fat.

3

Stir the broth and black pepper into skillet. Bring to boiling; reduce heat. Simmer, uncovered, for 5 minutes. Remove from heat. Pour over pasta; add parsley. Toss gently to coat. Transfer to a warm serving dish.

Nutrition Facts per serving: 397 calories, 18 g total fat, 94 mg cholesterol, 713 mg sodium, 38 g carbohydrate, 24 g protein.

PASTA WITH PEPPERONI MARINARA

With pepperoni and a zesty sauce, this hearty dish is sure to become a family favorite.

Start to Finish: 30 minutes **Makes:** 6 servings

1 pound dried penne (mostaccioli) or
  cut ziti
1 cup sliced onion
2 tablespoons olive oil
1 teaspoon bottled minced garlic
$1/4$ teaspoon crushed red pepper
1 14-ounce jar marinara sauce

$1/2$ cup pepperoni cut into thin
  bite-size strips
$1/4$ teaspoon salt
$1/4$ teaspoon freshly ground black
  pepper
$1/4$ cup snipped fresh parsley
  Fresh parsley sprigs (optional)

1

Cook pasta according to package directions. Drain. Cover and keep warm.

2

Meanwhile, in a large skillet cook onion in hot oil over medium-high heat about 8 minutes or until golden brown. Add garlic and crushed red pepper; cook for 15 seconds. Stir in the marinara sauce and pepperoni. Stir in salt and black pepper.

3

In a serving bowl toss the pepperoni mixture with the hot pasta and the snipped parsley. If desired, garnish with parsley sprigs.

Nutrition Facts per serving: 410 calories, 11 g total fat, 6 mg cholesterol, 658 mg sodium, 66 g carbohydrate, 13 g protein.

FETTUCCINE STRAW AND HAY WITH PARMESAN

Plain white fettuccine and colorful spinach fettuccine give this saucy dish a distinctive appearance reminiscent of brown straw mixed with green hay.

Start to Finish: 30 minutes **Makes:** 6 servings

8 ounces dried fettuccine or linguine
8 ounces dried spinach fettuccine or linguine
$1/2$ cup finely chopped onion
1 tablespoon butter or margarine
1 cup chicken broth
$1/4$ teaspoon salt
$1/4$ teaspoon freshly ground black pepper

1 cup whipping cream
1 cup loose-pack frozen peas
4 ounces thinly sliced prosciutto, cut into thin strips
$1/2$ cup finely shredded Parmesan cheese (2 ounces)
Shredded Parmesan cheese

1

Cook pasta according to package directions. Drain. Cover and keep warm.

2

Meanwhile, for sauce, in a large skillet cook onion in hot butter or margarine for 3 minutes. Carefully add the chicken broth, salt, and pepper; cook until reduced to $1/2$ cup. Add whipping cream; boil about 5 minutes or until thickened. Stir in peas and cook about 1 minute more or until heated through.

3

In a large serving bowl toss sauce with hot pasta, prosciutto, and the $1/2$ cup Parmesan cheese. If desired, garnish with additional Parmesan cheese.

Nutrition Facts per serving: 545 calories, 25 g total fat, 152 mg cholesterol, 854 mg sodium, 59 g carbohydrate, 21 g protein.

MEDITERRANEAN MOSTACCIOLI

Mediterranean cooks are experts at making a little meat go a long way—as evidenced by this hearty main dish.

Start to Finish: 30 minutes **Makes:** 4 servings

6 ounces dried penne (mostaccioli) or gemelli
$^1/_2$ of a medium eggplant, cubed (about 3 cups)
2 cups halved sliced zucchini
8 ounces ground lamb or ground beef
2 14$^1/_2$-ounce cans diced tomatoes with basil, oregano, and garlic

$^1/_2$ cup raisins
$^1/_4$ cup snipped fresh basil
$^1/_2$ teaspoon ground cinnamon
2 tablespoons balsamic vinegar
2 tablespoons crumbled feta cheese (optional)

1
Cook pasta according to package directions, adding eggplant and zucchini for the last 2 minutes of cooking. Drain. Cover and keep warm.

2
Meanwhile, for sauce, in a large skillet cook meat until browned; drain off fat. Stir in undrained tomatoes, raisins, basil, and cinnamon. Bring to boiling; reduce heat. Cover and simmer for 5 minutes, stirring once or twice. Remove from heat; stir in balsamic vinegar.

3
Transfer pasta mixture to a warm serving platter. Spoon sauce over pasta mixture. If desired, sprinkle with crumbled feta cheese.

Nutrition Facts per serving: 432 calories, 8 g total fat, 38 mg cholesterol, 939 mg sodium, 72 g carbohydrate, 18 g protein.

SHANGHAI PORK LO MEIN

Look for the thin Japanese noodles called somen in an Asian food market.

Start to Finish: 20 minutes   **Makes:** 4 servings

3 cups dried somen or fine egg
   noodles (6 ounces)

2 teaspoons cooking oil

8 ounces pork tenderloin, halved
   lengthwise and cut into
   $1/4$-inch slices

2 cups sliced bok choy

$3/4$ cup reduced-sodium chicken broth

$1/4$ cup orange juice

3 tablespoons reduced-sodium soy
   sauce

2 teaspoons toasted sesame oil

$1/4$ to $1/2$ teaspoon crushed red pepper

1 11-ounce can mandarin orange
   sections, drained, or 2 large
   oranges, peeled, sectioned, and
   seeded

1
Cook noodles according to package directions. Drain. Cover and keep warm.

2
Meanwhile, heat oil in a wok or large skillet over medium-high heat. (Add more oil as necessary during cooking.) Stir-fry pork in hot oil for 3 minutes. Add bok choy; cook and stir about 2 minutes more or until the pork is done and the bok choy is crisp-tender.

3
Add chicken broth, orange juice, soy sauce, sesame oil, and crushed red pepper to wok; bring to boiling. Add cooked noodles. Toss to coat all ingredients. Cook for 1 minute, stirring occasionally. Stir in the orange sections.

Nutrition Facts per serving: 323 calories, 7 g total fat, 40 mg cholesterol, 1,337 mg sodium, 45 g carbohydrate, 20 g protein.

SPAETZLE WITH CARAMELIZED ONIONS

German cooks make tiny dumplings known as spaetzle by pressing the dough through a spaetzle sieve or colander. This recipe shortcuts the preparation by relying on dried spaetzle.

Start to Finish: 30 minutes **Makes:** 4 servings

2 large onions, cut into thin wedges
2 tablespoons margarine or butter
3/4 cup yellow, orange, and/or red sweet pepper cut into bite-size strips
4 teaspoons brown sugar
1 tablespoon cider vinegar
1/3 cup chicken broth
1/3 cup half-and-half or light cream

1 tablespoon snipped fresh dill
1/8 teaspoon ground black pepper
2 cups dried spaetzle, kluski-style egg noodles, or medium noodles (4 ounces)
2 cups halved fresh Brussels sprouts
1 cup cooked pork or ham cut into bite-size strips

1

In a covered large skillet cook onions in hot margarine or butter over medium-low heat for 13 to 15 minutes or until onions are tender. Uncover; add sweet pepper strips, brown sugar, and vinegar. Cook and stir over medium-high heat for 4 to 5 minutes or until onions are golden. Stir in the chicken broth, half-and-half or light cream, dill, and black pepper. Boil gently until mixture is thickened.

2

Meanwhile, cook spaetzle or noodles according to package directions, adding Brussels sprouts to the water with the spaetzle. Drain and return to saucepan. Add onion mixture and pork or ham to saucepan. Cook and stir over low heat until spaetzle are well coated and mixture is heated through.

Nutrition Facts per serving: 374 calories, 15 g total fat, 91 mg cholesterol, 279 mg sodium, 42 g carbohydrate, 20 g protein.

SUMMER PASTA WITH PORK

Fresh summer vegetables take center stage in this memorable dish.

Start to Finish: 30 minutes **Makes:** 4 servings

2 tablespoons dried mushrooms (such as shiitake or porcini)

¼ cup dried tomatoes (not oil-packed)

3 cups dried trenne or large bow ties (farfalle) (6 ounces)

2 cups fresh green beans cut into 1-inch pieces

1 medium yellow summer squash, halved and sliced

1 cup milk

¾ cup chicken broth

1 green onion, sliced

1 tablespoon cornstarch

Lemon-pepper seasoning

Salt

1 pound boneless pork loin chops, cut ¾ to 1 inch thick

1 tablespoon olive oil

1

Soak mushrooms and tomatoes in enough boiling water to cover for 5 minutes. Drain and snip, discarding mushroom stems. Set aside.

2

Cook pasta according to package directions, adding green beans to the water with the pasta. Add squash for the last 2 minutes of cooking. Drain. Cover and keep warm.

3

Meanwhile, in a medium bowl stir together the milk, chicken broth, green onion, cornstarch, ½ teaspoon lemon-pepper seasoning, and ¼ teaspoon salt; set aside.

4

Season pork lightly with additional lemon-pepper seasoning and additional salt. In a medium skillet cook pork in hot oil over medium heat for 8 to 12 minutes or until juices run clear (160°F), turning once halfway through cooking. Remove meat from skillet; cut into thin bite-size strips. Keep warm.

5

For sauce, drain fat from skillet. Stir cornstarch mixture; pour into skillet. Cook and stir until thickened and bubbly, scraping up any brown bits from bottom of skillet. Reduce heat; cook for 2 minutes more. Stir in soaked mushrooms and tomatoes.

6

Divide pasta mixture among 4 dinner plates. Arrange pork on pasta; spoon sauce over all. If desired, sprinkle with additional lemon-pepper seasoning.

Nutrition Facts per serving: 435 calories, 20 g total fat, 110 mg cholesterol, 659 mg sodium, 43 g carbohydrate, 26 g protein.

GREEK-STYLE PASTA SKILLET

Greek cooks favor lamb for their meat-and-pasta dishes, but ground beef is equally good.

Prep: 15 minutes   **Cook:** 15 minutes   **Makes:** 4 servings

12 ounces ground lamb or ground beef
1 medium onion, chopped
1 $14^{1}/_{2}$-ounce can diced tomatoes
1 $5^{1}/_{2}$-ounce can ($^{2}/_{3}$ cup) tomato juice
$^{1}/_{2}$ cup water
$^{1}/_{2}$ teaspoon instant beef bouillon granules

$^{1}/_{2}$ teaspoon ground cinnamon
$^{1}/_{8}$ teaspoon garlic powder
1 cup dried medium shell macaroni or elbow macaroni (about 3 ounces)
1 cup loose-pack frozen cut green beans
$^{1}/_{2}$ cup crumbled feta cheese (2 ounces)

1

In a large skillet cook ground lamb or beef and onion until meat is browned. Drain off fat. Stir in undrained tomatoes, tomato juice, the water, bouillon granules, cinnamon, and garlic powder. Bring to boiling.

2

Stir uncooked macaroni and green beans into meat mixture. Return to boiling; reduce heat. Cover and simmer about 15 minutes or until macaroni and green beans are tender. Sprinkle with feta cheese.

Nutrition Facts per serving: 362 calories, 16 g total fat, 70 mg cholesterol, 647 mg sodium, 33 g carbohydrate, 22 g protein.

CHICKEN AND PASTA TOSS

If you have a wok, use it instead of a large skillet.

Start to Finish: 30 minutes **Makes:** 4 servings

8 ounces dried angel hair pasta
  (capellini) or vermicelli
1 tablespoon olive oil
1 cup thinly sliced carrots
1 cup chopped broccoli
1 small onion, sliced
12 ounces skinless, boneless chicken
  breasts, cut into bite-size pieces

$^1/_3$ cup chicken broth
$^1/_4$ cup dry white wine
$^1/_2$ cup chopped oil-packed dried
  tomatoes, drained
1 teaspoon dried basil, crushed
$^1/_4$ teaspoon dried thyme, crushed
1 clove garlic, minced
  Grated Parmesan cheese

1

Cook pasta according to package directions. Drain. Cover and keep warm.

2

Meanwhile, heat oil in a large skillet over medium-high heat. (Add more oil as necessary during cooking.) Stir-fry carrots in hot oil for 2 minutes. Add broccoli and onion; stir-fry for 2 to 3 minutes more or until crisp-tender. Remove vegetables from skillet.

3

Add chicken pieces to hot skillet; stir-fry for 4 to 5 minutes or until no longer pink. Stir in broth, white wine, tomatoes, basil, thyme, and garlic; cook and stir for 1 minute. Return vegetables to skillet; add pasta. Toss gently about 1 minute more or until heated through. Sprinkle with Parmesan cheese.

Nutrition Facts per serving: 395 calories, 10 g total fat, 47 mg cholesterol, 235 mg sodium, 48 g carbohydrate, 27 g protein.

LEMON-PEPPER PASTA AND CHICKEN

If you can't find lemon-pepper pasta, use plain linguine or fettuccine and toss the cooked pasta with ¼ teaspoon ground black pepper and ¼ teaspoon finely shredded lemon peel.

Start to Finish: 20 minutes **Makes:** 4 servings

8 ounces dried lemon-pepper linguine or plain fettuccine

1 cup shelled fresh or loose-pack frozen baby peas

3 tablespoons olive oil

12 ounces skinless, boneless chicken breasts, cut into thin bite-size strips

1 medium red onion, cut into thin wedges

1 tablespoon snipped fresh marjoram or 1 teaspoon dried marjoram, crushed

4 cloves garlic, sliced

½ teaspoon salt

1 tablespoon lemon juice

1

Cook pasta according to package directions, adding peas for the last 1 minute of cooking. Drain pasta mixture; toss with 1 tablespoon of the olive oil. Cover and keep warm.

2

Meanwhile, in a large skillet cook chicken, onion, dried marjoram (if using), garlic, and salt in remaining hot oil for 3 to 4 minutes or until chicken is no longer pink, stirring often. Stir in lemon juice. Cook and stir for 1 minute more, scraping up brown bits.

3

Gently toss hot cooked pasta with chicken mixture and fresh marjoram (if using).

Nutrition Facts per serving: 446 calories, 14 g total fat, 45 mg cholesterol, 311 mg sodium, 54 g carbohydrate, 26 g protein.

SUMMER CHICKEN AND MUSHROOM PASTA

When a warm summer evening calls for a light, fresh-testing meal, this garlic-infused medley is a tasty solution.

Start to Finish: 30 minutes **Makes:** 6 servings

8 ounces dried penne pasta (mostaccioli)

12 ounces skinless, boneless chicken breast halves, cut into bite-size strips

$1/4$ teaspoon salt

$1/8$ teaspoon freshly ground black pepper

2 tablespoons olive oil or cooking oil

3 large cloves garlic, minced

3 cups sliced fresh mushrooms

1 medium onion, thinly sliced

$1/2$ cup chicken broth

$1/4$ cup dry white wine

1 cup yellow baby pear tomatoes or cherry tomatoes, halved

$1/4$ cup shredded fresh basil

3 tablespoons snipped fresh oregano

$1/8$ teaspoon freshly ground black pepper

1

Cook pasta according to package directions. Drain; return pasta to saucepan. Cover and keep warm.

2

Meanwhile, sprinkle chicken with salt and $1/8$ teaspoon pepper. In a large skillet heat 1 tablespoon of the oil over medium-high heat. Add chicken and garlic. Cook and stir for 3 to 4 minutes or until chicken is tender and no longer pink. Remove from skillet. Cover and keep warm.

3

Add the remaining oil to skillet. Add mushrooms and onion. Cook and stir just until vegetables are tender. Carefully add chicken broth and wine. Bring to boiling; reduce heat. Boil gently about 2 minutes or until liquid is reduced by half. Remove skillet from heat.

4

Add cooked pasta, tomatoes, basil, and oregano to skillet. Toss gently to coat all ingredients. Transfer chicken mixture to a serving bowl; sprinkle with $1/8$ teaspoon pepper.

Nutrition Facts per serving: 299 calories, 8 g total fat, 37 mg cholesterol, 249 mg sodium, 33 g carbohydrate, 22 g protein.

CHICKEN AND PENNE WITH BASIL SAUCE

Fresh basil is a key ingredient in this well-seasoned main dish.

Start to Finish: 25 minutes   **Makes:** 4 servings

1$\frac{1}{4}$ cups reduced-sodium chicken broth
4 teaspoons cornstarch
$\frac{1}{8}$ teaspoon ground black pepper
2 cups dried penne (mostaccioli)
   or 1$\frac{1}{2}$ cups dried elbow macaroni
   (6 ounces)
   Nonstick cooking spray
1 medium red sweet pepper, cut into
   thin strips
1 medium yellow or green sweet
   pepper, cut into thin strips

3 cloves garlic, minced
1 tablespoon cooking oil
12 ounces skinless, boneless chicken
   breasts, cut into 1-inch cubes
$\frac{1}{4}$ cup lightly packed fresh basil
   leaves, cut into thin shreds
2 tablespoons shredded Parmesan
   cheese
   Fresh basil sprigs (optional)

1

In a small bowl stir together chicken broth, cornstarch, and black pepper. Set aside.

2

Cook pasta according to package directions, except omit any oil or salt. Drain. Cover and keep warm.

3

Meanwhile, coat an unheated large skillet with nonstick cooking spray. Preheat over medium heat. Add sweet peppers and garlic; stir-fry for 2 to 3 minutes or until sweet peppers are crisp-tender. Remove from skillet. Add the oil to skillet; increase heat to medium-high. Add chicken; stir-fry for 3 to 4 minutes or until chicken is no longer pink. Stir broth mixture; add to skillet. Cook and stir until thickened and bubbly.

4

Return sweet peppers to skillet; add the basil shreds. Cook and stir for 2 minutes more. Toss with hot pasta. Sprinkle with Parmesan cheese. If desired, garnish with basil sprigs.

Nutrition Facts per serving: 330 calories, 8 g total fat, 47 mg cholesterol, 282 mg sodium, 39 g carbohydrate, 24 g protein.

FETTUCCINE WITH SWEET PEPPERS AND ONIONS

To make Romano cheese shavings, firmly pull a vegetable peeler or a cheese shaver over the edge of a block of Romano.

Start to Finish: 25 minutes **Makes:** 4 servings

$1/2$ cup chicken broth

1 teaspoon cornstarch

1 16-ounce package frozen sweet pepper stir-fry vegetables (yellow, green, and red sweet peppers and onions)

1 9-ounce package refrigerated fettuccine or linguine

1 tablespoon olive oil

12 ounces skinless, boneless chicken breasts, cut into bite-size pieces

2 teaspoons bottled minced garlic

$1/4$ to $1/2$ teaspoon crushed red pepper

$1/2$ cup chopped tomatoes

$1/4$ cup snipped fresh basil

Shaved Romano cheese

Fresh basil leaves (optional)

1

In a small bowl stir together chicken broth and cornstarch; set aside.

2

Bring a Dutch oven of salted water to boiling. Add frozen pepper mixture and pasta. Return to boiling and cook for 2 minutes or just until pasta is tender. Drain and return to Dutch oven. Toss with 1 teaspoon of the oil. Keep pasta warm.

3

Meanwhile, in a large skillet cook chicken, garlic, and crushed red pepper in remaining oil over medium-high heat for 2 to 3 minutes or until chicken is no longer pink, stirring often. Push chicken to side of skillet. Stir cornstarch mixture; add to center of skillet. Cook and stir until thickened and bubbly. Cook and stir for 2 minutes more. Stir to coat with sauce.

4

Remove chicken and sauce from heat; toss with cooked pasta mixture, tomatoes, and snipped basil. Serve topped with shaved Romano cheese. If desired, garnish with basil leaves.

Nutrition Facts per serving: 389 calories, 9 g total fat, 96 mg cholesterol, 261 mg sodium, 46 g carbohydrate, 28 g protein.

ANGEL HAIR PASTA WITH CHICKEN AND SHRIMP

A trio of vegetables complements the saucy chicken and shrimp mixture.

Start to Finish: 30 minutes **Makes:** 4 servings

4 ounces fresh or frozen peeled and
   deveined medium shrimp
1/2 cup reduced-sodium chicken broth
2 tablespoons reduced-sodium soy
   sauce
2 teaspoons cornstarch
1/2 teaspoon ground ginger
6 ounces dried angel hair pasta
   (capellini) or linguine
   Nonstick cooking spray

1 to 2 teaspoons cooking oil (optional)
1/2 cup green onions cut into 1/2-inch
   pieces
2 cloves garlic, minced
1 medium yellow summer squash,
   sliced
1 small red or green sweet pepper,
   cut into thin strips
8 ounces skinless, boneless chicken
   breasts, cut into 3/4-inch pieces

1

Thaw shrimp, if frozen. Rinse shrimp; pat dry. In a small bowl combine the chicken broth, soy sauce, cornstarch, and ginger. Set aside.

2

Cook pasta according to package directions, except omit any oil or salt. Drain. Cover and keep warm.

3

Meanwhile, coat an unheated large skillet with nonstick cooking spray. (Add oil as necessary during cooking.) Preheat skillet over medium heat. Add green onions and garlic; stir-fry for 1 minute. Remove from skillet. Add summer squash to skillet; stir-fry for 1 1/2 minutes. Add sweet pepper; stir-fry for 1 1/2 minutes more or until vegetables are crisp-tender. Remove vegetables from skillet.

4

Add chicken and shrimp to skillet; stir-fry for 3 to 4 minutes or until chicken is no longer pink and shrimp turn opaque. Push chicken and shrimp from the center of the skillet. Stir broth mixture; add to center of the skillet. Cook and stir until thickened and bubbly. Return all of the cooked vegetables to skillet; stir all ingredients together to coat with sauce. Cook and stir about 1 minute more or until heated through. Serve hot chicken mixture over pasta.

Nutrition Facts per serving: 268 calories, 5 g total fat, 110 mg cholesterol, 413 mg sodium, 33 g carbohydrate, 23 g protein.

STROGANOFF-STYLE CHICKEN

This version of stroganoff uses chicken and light sour cream for a rich-tasting dish with less fat and calories than the classic.

Start to Finish: 25 minutes **Makes:** 5 servings

12 ounces dried medium noodles or fettuccine
  Nonstick cooking spray
2 cups sliced fresh mushrooms
1/2 cup chopped onion
2 teaspoons cooking oil (optional)
12 ounces skinless, boneless chicken breasts, cut into 1-inch cubes

1 8-ounce carton light dairy sour cream
2 tablespoons all-purpose flour
1 teaspoon paprika
1/4 teaspoon salt
1/2 cup reduced-sodium chicken broth

1
Cook noodles or fettuccine according to package directions. Drain. Cover and keep warm.

2
Meanwhile, coat an unheated large skillet with nonstick cooking spray. Preheat over medium heat. Add mushrooms and onion; cook until onion is nearly tender.

3
If needed, add oil to skillet. Add chicken cubes and cook for 3 to 4 minutes or until chicken is tender and no longer pink.

4
In a small bowl stir together the sour cream, flour, paprika, and salt; stir in chicken broth. Add to skillet. Cook and stir until slightly thickened and bubbly. Cook and stir for 1 minute more. Serve over hot cooked noodles or fettuccine.

Nutrition Facts per serving: 308 calories, 7 g total fat, 79 mg cholesterol, 257 mg sodium, 39 g carbohydrate, 23 g protein.

HOISIN-GLAZED TURKEY MEDALLIONS

Orange marmalade, hoisin sauce, soy sauce, and fresh ginger meld into a sweet-and-savory glaze for the turkey and pasta. (Pictured on page 11.)

Start to Finish: 25 minutes **Makes:** 2 servings

4 ounces dried spinach fettuccine, plain fettuccine, or linguine

1 8-ounce turkey breast tenderloin

1 tablespoon cooking oil

1/4 cup orange marmalade

2 tablespoons hoisin sauce

1 1/2 teaspoons reduced-sodium soy sauce

1/2 teaspoon grated fresh ginger

2 tablespoons sliced almonds, toasted

1 green onion, cut into very thin strips

1
Cook pasta according to package directions. Drain. Cover and keep warm.

2
Meanwhile, cut turkey crosswise into 1/2-inch slices. In a large nonstick skillet cook turkey in hot oil over medium-high heat for 3 to 4 minutes or until turkey is tender and no longer pink, turning once. Remove turkey; cover and keep warm. If necessary, drain off fat.

3
For sauce, in a small bowl stir together the orange marmalade, hoisin sauce, soy sauce, and ginger. Add to skillet. Cook and stir until bubbly. Cook, uncovered, about 1 minute or until slightly thickened. Remove from heat. Return turkey to skillet, turning to coat with sauce.

4
To serve, divide the pasta between 2 dinner plates. Arrange the turkey slices on top of pasta. Drizzle with the sauce and sprinkle with almonds. Top with green onion strips.

Nutrition Facts per serving: 539 calories, 14 g total fat, 113 mg cholesterol, 475 mg sodium, 68 g carbohydrate, 37 g protein.

PASTA WITH SPINACH AND SMOKED SAUSAGE

To make sure the fresh spinach doesn't get mushy, cook it just until it starts to wilt.

Start to Finish: 25 minutes **Makes:** 4 servings

- 3 cups dried medium bow ties or 1½ cups dried elbow macaroni (6 ounces)
- 4 ounces cooked smoked turkey or chicken sausage links
- 1 large leek, cut into ¼-inch slices
- 2 cloves garlic, minced
- 1 teaspoon olive oil
- ⅔ cup reduced-sodium chicken broth

- ½ of a 7-ounce jar roasted red sweet peppers, drained and cut into thin bite-size strips
- 8 cups torn fresh spinach
- ¼ cup snipped fresh basil or 1 tablespoon dried basil, crushed
- ¼ cup finely shredded Parmesan cheese (1 ounce)
- ¼ teaspoon cracked black pepper

1

Cook pasta according to package directions, except omit any oil or salt. Drain; return pasta to saucepan. Cover and keep warm.

2

Meanwhile, cut the sausage lengthwise into quarters. Cut into ¼-inch pieces. In a large skillet cook leek and garlic in hot oil until leek is tender. Stir in sausage, chicken broth, and roasted peppers. Bring to boiling; reduce heat. Add spinach. Cook, stirring frequently, for 1 to 2 minutes or just until spinach starts to wilt. Remove from heat.

3

Add spinach mixture, basil, Parmesan cheese, and black pepper to pasta in saucepan. Toss to coat.

Nutrition Facts per serving: 265 calories, 8 g total fat, 61 mg cholesterol, 440 mg sodium, 34 g carbohydrate, 14 g protein.

SAUCY FISH FILLETS WITH PASTA

For a dramatic presentation, use a mixture of spinach fettuccine and plain fettuccine.

Start to Finish: 30 minutes **Makes:** 4 servings

- 1 pound fresh or frozen fish fillets (such as orange roughy, cod, or halibut)
- 12 ounces dried spinach or plain fettuccine or linguine
- 1 medium onion, chopped
- 1 tablespoon olive oil
- 1 14$\frac{1}{2}$-ounce can diced tomatoes with basil, oregano, and garlic

- $\frac{1}{3}$ cup water
- 1 tablespoon capers, drained and chopped
- $\frac{1}{8}$ teaspoon pepper
- 2 tablespoons cold water
- 1 tablespoon cornstarch
- 2 tablespoons thinly sliced, pitted ripe olives
- Fresh parsley sprigs (optional)

1

Thaw fish, if frozen. Separate fillets or cut into 4 serving-size pieces. Rinse fish; pat dry. Measure thickness of fish.

2

Cook pasta according to package directions. Drain. Cover and keep warm.

3

For sauce, in a large skillet cook onion in hot oil for 4 to 5 minutes or until tender. Stir in undrained tomatoes, the $\frac{1}{3}$ cup water, capers, and pepper. Bring to boiling; reduce heat. Cover and simmer for 5 minutes.

4

Add fish to sauce, spooning some of the sauce over the fish. Return to boiling; reduce heat. Cover and simmer just until fish flakes easily with a fork. (Allow 4 to 6 minutes for each $\frac{1}{2}$-inch thickness of fish.) Remove fish from skillet with slotted spatula, reserving tomato mixture in skillet. Cover fish and keep warm.

5

In a small bowl stir together the 1 tablespoon cold water and cornstarch; stir into the tomato mixture. Cook and stir until thickened and bubbly. Cook and stir for 2 minutes more.

6

Divide pasta among 4 dinner plates. Top with fish and tomato mixture. Sprinkle with olives. If desired, garnish with parsley sprigs.

Nutrition Facts per serving: 500 calories, 6 g total fat, 48 mg cholesterol, 723 mg sodium, 77 g carbohydrate, 34 g protein.

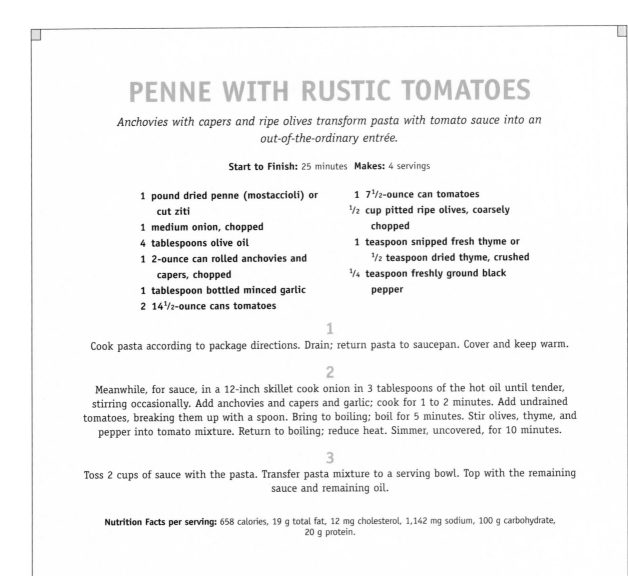

PENNE WITH RUSTIC TOMATOES

Anchovies with capers and ripe olives transform pasta with tomato sauce into an out-of-the-ordinary entrée.

Start to Finish: 25 minutes **Makes:** 4 servings

1 pound dried penne (mostaccioli) or cut ziti
1 medium onion, chopped
4 tablespoons olive oil
1 2-ounce can rolled anchovies and capers, chopped
1 tablespoon bottled minced garlic
2 14$^1/_2$-ounce cans tomatoes

1 7$^1/_2$-ounce can tomatoes
$^1/_2$ cup pitted ripe olives, coarsely chopped
1 teaspoon snipped fresh thyme or $^1/_2$ teaspoon dried thyme, crushed
$^1/_4$ teaspoon freshly ground black pepper

1

Cook pasta according to package directions. Drain; return pasta to saucepan. Cover and keep warm.

2

Meanwhile, for sauce, in a 12-inch skillet cook onion in 3 tablespoons of the hot oil until tender, stirring occasionally. Add anchovies and capers and garlic; cook for 1 to 2 minutes. Add undrained tomatoes, breaking them up with a spoon. Bring to boiling; boil for 5 minutes. Stir olives, thyme, and pepper into tomato mixture. Return to boiling; reduce heat. Simmer, uncovered, for 10 minutes.

3

Toss 2 cups of sauce with the pasta. Transfer pasta mixture to a serving bowl. Top with the remaining sauce and remaining oil.

Nutrition Facts per serving: 658 calories, 19 g total fat, 12 mg cholesterol, 1,142 mg sodium, 100 g carbohydrate, 20 g protein.

BOW TIES WITH SCALLOPS AND CHARD SAUCE

Next time you're looking for an elegant yet easy entrée for two, try this special dish.

Start to Finish: 20 minutes **Makes:** 2 servings

6 ounces fresh or frozen bay scallops
   (about 1 cup)
2 cups dried large bow ties (farfalle)
   or corkscrew macaroni (rotini)
   (about 4 ounces)
4 medium plum tomatoes, diced

2 cloves garlic, minced
2 teaspoons olive oil
$^2/_3$ cup chicken broth
1 cup shredded Swiss chard
   Shredded Parmesan cheese
   Fresh oregano leaves (optional)

1
Thaw scallops, if frozen. Rinse scallops; pat dry. Cook pasta according to package directions. Drain. Cover and keep warm.

2
Meanwhile, in a large skillet cook tomatoes and garlic in hot oil over medium heat for 3 to 4 minutes or until tomatoes are soft. Stir in the chicken broth. Bring to boiling; reduce heat. Simmer, uncovered, for 1 minute. Add scallops; cook about 1 minute more or until scallops turn opaque.

3
Toss pasta and Swiss chard into scallop mixture. To serve, sprinkle with Parmesan cheese. If desired, garnish with oregano.

Nutrition Facts per serving: 409 calories, 10 g total fat, 88 mg cholesterol, 529 mg sodium, 51 g carbohydrate, 28 g protein.

SHRIMP AND TOMATOES WITH PASTA

If you can't find plum tomatoes, use regular tomatoes instead. You'll need about 3 small or 2 medium tomatoes to get 1²/₃ cups chopped tomatoes.

Start to Finish: 25 minutes **Makes:** 4 servings

- 1 12-ounce package frozen peeled and deveined shrimp
- 1 9-ounce package refrigerated spinach or plain fettuccine or plain linguine
- 1 medium onion, chopped
- 1 teaspoon bottled minced garlic
- 1 tablespoon olive oil or cooking oil

- 4 medium plum tomatoes, chopped (about 1²/₃ cups)
- 2 teaspoons snipped fresh tarragon or ¹/₂ teaspoon dried tarragon, crushed
- ¹/₄ teaspoon coarsely ground black pepper

1

In a large saucepan cook the shrimp with the fettuccine according to fettuccine package directions. Drain; return to saucepan. Cover and keep warm.

2

Meanwhile, in a medium saucepan cook onion and garlic in hot oil until onion is tender. Stir in plum tomatoes, tarragon, and pepper. Cook over low heat, stirring occasionally, for 2 to 3 minutes or until hot.

3

Add tomato mixture to fettuccine mixture in saucepan. Toss to coat.

Nutrition Facts per serving: 277 calories, 5 g total fat, 131 mg cholesterol, 173 mg sodium, 37 g carbohydrate, 20 g protein.

HERBED SHRIMP-PASTA MEDLEY

If you can't find baby pattypan squash, use 6 ounces sliced yellow summer squash.

Start to Finish: 25 minutes **Makes:** 4 servings

8 ounces fresh or frozen small shrimp
  in shells

8 ounces dried garlic-basil or
  tomato-basil fettuccine or linguine

6 ounces baby pattypan squash
  (yellow or green), halved or
  quartered

1/2 of a medium red onion, cut into
  thin wedges

2 cloves garlic, minced

1 tablespoon olive oil

1 cup evaporated fat-free milk

1/2 teaspoon bottled hot pepper sauce

4 ounces goat cheese (chèvre), cut up

3 tablespoons snipped fresh basil

2 teaspoons finely shredded lemon
  peel

1 teaspoon snipped fresh mint

1/4 teaspoon salt

1/4 teaspoon coarsely ground black
  pepper

1 small head radicchio, torn, or 1/2 of
  a small head curly endive, torn
  (about 4 ounces)

Fresh basil leaves (optional)

Cherry tomatoes, halved (optional)

1
Thaw shrimp, if frozen. Peel and devein shrimp, leaving tails intact. Rinse shrimp; pat dry. Cook pasta according to package directions. Drain. Cover and keep warm.

2
Meanwhile, in a medium skillet cook the squash, onion, and garlic in hot oil about 3 minutes or until onion and squash begin to soften. Add the shrimp and cook for 2 to 3 minutes more or until shrimp turn opaque.

3
Reduce heat; stir in evaporated milk and hot pepper sauce. Remove from heat. Stir in cooked pasta and cheese; stir until cheese is melted. Stir in snipped basil, lemon peel, mint, salt, and pepper. Stir in radicchio or endive just until wilted. If desired, garnish with basil leaves and cherry tomatoes.

Nutrition Facts per serving: 435 calories, 11 g total fat, 80 mg cholesterol, 400 mg sodium, 55 g carbohydrate, 27 g protein.

FETTUCCINE WITH ARTICHOKES AND BASIL

Serve this tasty combo with tomato slices and crusty bread for a light lunch or supper.

Start to Finish: 25 minutes **Makes:** 3 servings

- 4 ounces dried fettuccine or fusilli, broken
- 1 9-ounce package frozen artichoke hearts, thawed, or one 14-ounce jar or can artichoke hearts, rinsed and drained
- 1½ cups chopped red or green sweet pepper

- ⅓ cup finely chopped onion
- 2 cloves garlic, minced
- 1 tablespoon olive oil
- ⅔ cup chopped seeded tomato
- ¼ cup snipped fresh basil or 2 teaspoons dried basil, crushed
- 2 tablespoons grated Parmesan cheese (optional)

1
Cook fettuccine according to package directions. Drain. Cover and keep warm.

2
Meanwhile, place frozen artichoke hearts in a colander under cold running water to separate. In a large skillet cook and stir artichokes, sweet pepper, onion, and garlic in hot oil over medium-high heat about 5 minutes or until vegetables are tender.

3
Stir in tomato and basil. Cook and stir about 2 minutes more or until heated through. Add vegetable mixture to fettuccine; toss gently to mix. If desired, sprinkle with Parmesan cheese.

Nutrition Facts per serving: 259 calories, 6 g total fat, 0 mg cholesterol, 62 mg sodium, 44 g carbohydrate, 8 g protein.

SUMMER SQUASH PRIMAVERA

Sprinkle on the Parmesan and toasted pine nuts just before serving.

Start to Finish: 25 minutes **Makes:** 4 to 6 servings

12 ounces dried linguine, corkscrew macaroni (rotini), or cut ziti
5 cloves garlic, minced
2 green onions, sliced
2 tablespoons olive oil
2 to 3 medium carrots, sliced
1 medium red sweet pepper, sliced
1 medium yellow sweet pepper, sliced

1 small zucchini, chopped
$1/4$ teaspoon salt
$1/4$ teaspoon ground black pepper
1 cup chicken broth
1 cup snipped fresh basil
$1/2$ cup shredded Parmesan cheese (2 ounces)
2 tablespoons pine nuts, toasted

1

Cook pasta according to package directions. Drain; return to saucepan. Cover and keep warm.

2

Meanwhile, in a large skillet cook garlic and green onions in hot oil for 30 seconds. Stir in carrots and sweet peppers. Cook and stir for 3 minutes more. Stir in chopped zucchini, salt, and black pepper. Cook and stir for 3 minutes more. Stir in chicken broth. Bring to boiling; reduce heat. Cover and simmer about 1 minute or just until vegetables are tender.

3

Stir vegetable mixture and basil into pasta; toss to coat. Sprinkle with cheese and pine nuts.

Nutrition Facts per serving: 513 calories, 15 g total fat, 13 mg cholesterol, 512 mg sodium, 75 g carbohydrate, 20 g protein.

PENNE WITH FENNEL

Set aside some of the feathery fennel leaves to use as a garnish.

Start to Finish: 30 minutes **Makes:** 4 servings

6 ounces dried penne (mostaccioli) or
  cut ziti
2 medium fennel bulbs
1 tablespoon olive oil or cooking oil
1 tablespoon margarine or butter
3 cloves garlic, minced
1/4 teaspoon crushed red pepper
1 cup red and/or green sweet pepper
  cut into thin bite-size strips

1 15-ounce can Great Northern beans,
  rinsed and drained
1/4 teaspoon dried thyme, crushed
  Cracked black pepper
1/4 cup shaved or shredded Parmesan
  cheese (1 ounce)

1

Cook pasta according to package directions. Drain; return pasta to saucepan. Cover and keep warm.

2

Meanwhile, cut off and discard upper stalks from fennel bulbs. If desired, reserve some of the leaves for garnish. Cut bulbs lengthwise into quarters. Remove and discard core. Cut fennel into thin strips.

3

In a large skillet heat oil and margarine or butter over medium-high heat. Add garlic and crushed red pepper; cook for 30 seconds. Add fennel to skillet; cook and stir for 5 minutes. Add sweet pepper strips; cook for 3 minutes. Add beans and thyme; cook for 2 minutes more.

4

Add fennel mixture to hot cooked pasta; toss gently. Season to taste with black pepper. Sprinkle with Parmesan cheese. If desired, garnish with reserved fennel leaves.

Nutrition Facts per serving: 349 calories, 9 g total fat, 5 mg cholesterol, 309 mg sodium, 53 g carbohydrate, 15 g protein.

SOUTHWESTERN PASTA

If mild suits your fancy, use only 1 teaspoon of the pickled jalapeño pepper.
To step up the heat a little, try 2 teaspoons.

Start to Finish: 30 minutes **Makes:** 2 servings

1$\frac{1}{3}$ cups dried wagon wheel macaroni
    (ruote) or penne (mostaccioli)
    (4 ounces)
1 tablespoon bottled minced garlic
1 tablespoon olive oil
4 medium tomatoes, seeded and
    chopped (about 3 cups), or one
    14$\frac{1}{2}$-ounce can diced tomatoes
4 oil-packed dried tomato halves,
    drained and chopped

$\frac{1}{4}$ cup dry sherry or chicken broth
1 to 2 teaspoons finely chopped
    pickled jalapeño pepper
2 tablespoons snipped fresh basil
2 tablespoons snipped fresh parsley
$\frac{1}{4}$ cup shredded cheddar cheese
    (1 ounce)
    Fresh chile peppers (optional)

1

Cook pasta according to package directions. Drain. Cover and keep warm.

2

Meanwhile, in a large skillet cook garlic in hot oil for 1 minute. Add fresh or undrained canned tomatoes, dried tomatoes, sherry or broth, and jalapeño pepper. Bring to boiling; reduce heat. Simmer, uncovered, for 10 minutes, stirring occasionally. Stir hot cooked pasta into mixture in skillet. Add basil and parsley; toss to combine. Sprinkle with cheese. If desired, garnish with chile peppers.

Nutrition Facts per serving: 472 calories, 15 g total fat, 15 mg cholesterol, 203 mg sodium, 64 g carbohydrate, 15 g protein.

PASTA ROSA VERDE

Rosy red tomatoes and bright green arugula contribute both color and flavor.

Start to Finish: 30 minutes **Makes:** 4 servings

8 ounces dried cut ziti or penne
(mostaccioli)
1 medium onion, thinly sliced
2 cloves garlic, minced
1 tablespoon olive oil
4 to 6 medium tomatoes, seeded and
coarsely chopped (3 cups)
1 teaspoon salt
1/2 teaspoon freshly ground black
pepper

1/4 teaspoon crushed red pepper
(optional)
3 cups arugula, watercress, and/or
fresh spinach, coarsely chopped
1/4 cup pine nuts or slivered almonds,
toasted
2 tablespoons crumbled Gorgonzola or
other blue cheese

1

Cook pasta according to package directions. Drain. Cover and keep warm.

2

Meanwhile, in a large skillet cook onion and garlic in hot oil over medium heat until onion is tender. Stir in tomatoes, salt, black pepper, and, if desired, crushed red pepper. Cook and stir over medium-high heat about 2 minutes or until tomatoes are warm and have released some of their juices. Stir in arugula, watercress, or spinach; heat just until wilted.

3

To serve, divide pasta among 4 serving bowls. Top with the tomato mixture. Sprinkle with toasted pine nuts and cheese.

Nutrition Facts per serving: 352 calories, 11 g total fat, 3 mg cholesterol, 610 mg sodium, 54 g carbohydrate, 12 g protein.

TRATTORIA-STYLE SPINACH FETTUCCINE

The savory sauce boasts double tomato flavor, from fresh and oil-packed dried tomatoes.

Start to Finish: 20 minutes **Makes:** 4 servings

1 9-ounce package refrigerated
   spinach fettuccine or herb linguine
2 tablespoons chopped shallot or
   green onion
1 tablespoon olive oil
4 small yellow and/or red tomatoes,
   chopped (2 cups)

1 medium carrot, finely chopped
$\frac{1}{4}$ cup oil-packed dried tomatoes,
   drained and snipped
$\frac{1}{2}$ cup crumbled garlic and herb feta
   cheese or peppercorn feta cheese
   (2 ounces)

1

Using kitchen scissors, cut fettuccine or linguine strands in half crosswise. Cook pasta according to package directions. Drain; return pasta to saucepan. Cover and keep warm.

2

Meanwhile, in a large skillet cook shallot or green onion in hot oil over medium heat for 30 seconds. Stir in fresh tomatoes, carrot, and dried tomatoes. Cook, covered, for 5 minutes, stirring once. Spoon tomato mixture over cooked pasta; toss gently. Sprinkle each serving with cheese.

Nutrition Facts per serving: 311 calories, 11 g total fat, 73 mg cholesterol, 250 mg sodium, 44 g carbohydrate, 13 g protein.

TERIYAKI PENNE

Trim a few more minutes off the prep time by using bottled grated fresh ginger and purchasing sliced mushrooms.

Start to Finish: 25 minutes **Makes:** 4 servings

$2^2/_3$ cups dried tomato-basil or plain penne (mostaccioli) or medium shell macaroni (about 8 ounces)

$^1/_2$ teaspoon grated fresh ginger

1 clove garlic, minced

1 tablespoon toasted sesame oil or cooking oil

3 cups packaged shredded broccoli (broccoli slaw mix)

2 cups sliced fresh mushrooms

$^1/_4$ cup bottled teriyaki sauce

$^1/_4$ cup thinly sliced green onions

1

Cook pasta according to package directions. Drain; return pasta to saucepan. Cover and keep warm.

2

Meanwhile, in a large skillet cook ginger and garlic in hot oil for 15 seconds. Stir in the shredded broccoli, mushrooms, and teriyaki sauce. Cook and stir about 5 minutes or until broccoli is crisp-tender.

3

To serve, add broccoli mixture to hot pasta; toss gently to combine. Sprinkle with green onions.

Nutrition Facts per serving: 286 calories, 5 g total fat, 0 mg cholesterol, 749 mg sodium, 50 g carbohydrate, 11 g protein.

SAUCEPAN FAVORITES

Simmered to perfection in a saucepan, these irresistible pasta dishes are as easy as they are delicious.

Pasta with Basil Cream Sauce
(see recipe, page 82)

ROASTED RED PEPPER SAUCE OVER TORTELLINI

Take your choice of meat- or cheese-filled tortellini or ravioli.

Start to Finish: 20 minutes   **Makes:** 3 servings

1 9-ounce package refrigerated meat-
   or cheese-filled tortellini or ravioli
1 12-ounce jar roasted red sweet
   peppers, drained
½ cup chopped onion
3 cloves garlic, minced

1 tablespoon margarine or butter
2 teaspoons snipped fresh thyme or
   ½ teaspoon dried thyme, crushed
2 teaspoons snipped fresh oregano or
   ¼ teaspoon dried oregano, crushed
1 teaspoon sugar

1

Cook pasta according to package directions. Drain; return to saucepan. Cover and keep warm.

2

Meanwhile, place roasted sweet peppers in a food processor bowl. Cover and process until smooth. Set aside.

3

For sauce, in a medium saucepan cook the onion and garlic in hot margarine or butter until tender. Add pureed peppers, thyme, oregano, and sugar. Cook and stir until heated through. Pour sauce over pasta; toss to coat.

Nutrition Facts per serving: 343 calories, 15 g total fat, 75 mg cholesterol, 298 mg sodium, 40 g carbohydrate, 14 g protein.

PASTA WITH BASIL CREAM SAUCE

When they're in season, feature fresh peas in this luscious pasta dish. Other times, use frozen peas. (Pictured on page 79.)

Start to Finish: 30 minutes   **Makes:** 4 servings

6 ounces dried campanelle, large bow ties (farfalle), or penne (mostaccioli)
1 cup shelled fresh peas*
1 12-ounce can (1½ cups) evaporated fat-free milk
1 tablespoon all-purpose flour
2 tablespoons snipped fresh basil

1 clove garlic, minced
¼ cup shredded Parmesan cheese (1 ounce)
2 ounces prosciutto, chopped
2 tablespoons shredded Parmesan cheese
Ground black pepper (optional)
Fresh basil leaves (optional)

1

Cook pasta according to package directions. Drain. Cover and keep warm.

2

Meanwhile, in a medium saucepan cook shelled peas in a small amount of boiling water for 10 minutes. Drain; return to saucepan. In a small bowl stir together the evaporated milk and flour; add to cooked peas in saucepan. Stir in snipped basil and garlic.

3

Cook and stir over medium heat until thickened and bubbly. Cook and stir for 1 minute more. Add the ¼ cup Parmesan cheese and the prosciutto; stir until cheese melts. Do not boil.

4

Pour prosciutto mixture over cooked pasta; toss gently to coat. Top with the 2 tablespoons Parmesan cheese; sprinkle with pepper. If desired, garnish with basil leaves.

Nutrition Facts per serving: 337 calories, 8 g total fat, 47 mg cholesterol, 478 mg sodium, 45 g carbohydrate, 21 g protein.

*Note: You can substitute ½ cup thawed frozen peas for the fresh peas. Cook pasta as above. In a medium saucepan stir together the evaporated fat-free milk and flour. Stir in snipped basil and garlic. Cook and stir until thickened and bubbly. Cook and stir for 1 minute more. Stir in the ¼ cup Parmesan cheese, the prosciutto, and the thawed peas; stir until cheese melts. Do not boil. Pour over pasta, toss, and serve as above.

FETTUCCINE WITH CREAMY HAM SAUCE

Remember this simple yet sensational entrée for your next dinner party.

Start to Finish: 25 minutes **Makes:** 4 servings

6 ounces dried fettuccine or linguine

2 cups broccoli or cauliflower florets

1 cup sliced fresh mushrooms

1 cup evaporated fat-free milk

2 teaspoons cornstarch

$1/2$ teaspoon dry mustard

$1/8$ teaspoon salt

$1/8$ teaspoon ground black pepper

$3/4$ cup shredded Swiss cheese
    (3 ounces)

1 cup low-fat, reduced-sodium cooked
    ham cut into thin strips
    (about 5 ounces)

1

Cook fettuccine according to package directions, except omit any oil or salt. Drain. Cover and keep warm.

2

Meanwhile, in a covered medium saucepan cook broccoli or cauliflower and mushrooms in a small amount of boiling water for 7 to 8 minutes or until vegetables are tender. Drain. Remove vegetables from saucepan. Cover and keep warm.

3

In the same saucepan stir together evaporated milk, cornstarch, dry mustard, salt, and pepper. Cook and stir over medium heat until thickened and bubbly. Add Swiss cheese; heat and stir until melted. Stir in ham and cooked vegetables; heat through. Spoon over hot pasta.

Nutrition Facts per serving: 365 calories, 8 g total fat, 36 mg cholesterol, 603 mg sodium, 48 g carbohydrate, 25 g protein.

HAM AND VEGETABLES WITH PENNE

Hearty yet healthful is the perfect description of this one-dish meal.

Start to Finish: 30 minutes **Makes:** 4 servings

1 1/3 cups dried penne (mostaccioli) or cut ziti (4 ounces)
2 cups sliced zucchini
1/2 cup sliced green onions
1/3 cup water
4 teaspoons cornstarch
2 teaspoons snipped fresh basil or 1/2 teaspoon dried basil, crushed
1/2 teaspoon snipped fresh marjoram or 1/4 teaspoon dried marjoram, crushed
1/8 teaspoon ground black pepper
1 cup evaporated fat-free milk
1/4 cup water
1 cup low-fat, reduced-sodium cooked ham cut into bite-size strips (about 5 ounces)
Fresh basil leaves (optional)

1

Cook pasta according to package directions, except omit any oil or salt. Drain. Cover and keep warm.

2

In a large saucepan combine zucchini, green onions, and the 1/3 cup water. Bring to boiling; reduce heat. Cover and simmer for 4 to 5 minutes or until vegetables are crisp-tender; drain well in a colander. Return vegetables to saucepan; cover and set aside.

3

Meanwhile, for sauce, in a small saucepan combine cornstarch, snipped or dried basil, marjoram, and pepper. Gradually stir in evaporated fat-free milk and the 1/4 cup water; add ham. Cook and stir until thickened and bubbly. Cook and stir for 2 minutes more. Add the ham mixture and the drained pasta to the vegetables in the saucepan. Heat through. If desired, garnish with fresh basil leaves.

Nutrition Facts per serving: 215 calories, 2 g total fat, 17 mg cholesterol, 465 mg sodium, 34 g carbohydrate, 15 g protein.

SOBA NOODLES
WITH SPRING VEGETABLES

Visit an Asian market to get the Japanese soba (buckwheat) noodles and the toasted sesame oil.

Start to Finish: 25 minutes **Makes:** 3 servings

1 14-ounce can vegetable or chicken broth
1 tablespoon finely chopped fresh ginger
1 tablespoon reduced-sodium soy sauce
4 ounces dried soba (buckwheat) noodles or whole wheat spaghetti, broken

1 medium carrot, thinly sliced
1 cup cubed cooked chicken or turkey (about 5 ounces)
1 cup shredded bok choy
1/2 cup halved fresh pea pods
1/3 cup sliced radishes or chopped daikon
1/2 teaspoon toasted sesame oil
Green onion strips

1

In a medium saucepan combine broth, ginger, and soy sauce. Bring to boiling; reduce heat. Cover and simmer for 5 minutes.

2

Stir in the soba noodles and carrot. (If using whole wheat spaghetti, stir in spaghetti and cook for 6 minutes before adding carrot.) Bring to boiling; reduce heat. Simmer, uncovered, about 4 minutes or until noodles and carrot are tender. Stir in chicken, bok choy, pea pods, radishes or daikon, and sesame oil. Heat through. Sprinkle each serving with green onion strips.

Nutrition Facts per serving: 276 calories, 8 g total fat, 39 mg cholesterol, 1,092 mg sodium, 37 g carbohydrate, 22 g protein.

TORTELLINI WITH TOMATO, CHICKEN, AND BASIL SAUCE

Next time you have a little chicken leftover, use it in this family-style dish.

Start to Finish: 30 minutes **Makes:** 3 servings

1 9-ounce package refrigerated cheese-filled tortellini or ravioli, or 4 ounces dried cheese-filled tortellini or ravioli

1 14$\frac{1}{2}$-ounce can pasta-style chunky tomatoes

1 cup cubed cooked chicken (about 5 ounces)

1 tablespoon snipped fresh basil or 1 teaspoon dried basil, crushed

$\frac{1}{4}$ teaspoon ground black pepper Shredded Parmesan or Romano cheese

1

In a large saucepan cook pasta according to package directions. Drain. Cover and keep warm.

2

Meanwhile, in a medium saucepan combine tomatoes, chicken, basil, and pepper; cook, stirring frequently, until boiling. Spoon over hot cooked pasta. Sprinkle with Parmesan or Romano cheese.

Nutrition Facts per serving: 408 calories, 11 g total fat, 91 mg cholesterol, 826 mg sodium, 47 g carbohydrate, 30 g protein.

BROCCOLI AND CHICKEN FETTUCCINE ALFREDO

Most any frozen vegetable—or a frozen vegetable combination—works as a substitute for the cut broccoli.

Start to Finish: 15 minutes **Makes:** 4 servings

1 9-ounce package refrigerated fettuccine or linguine
1½ cups loose-pack frozen cut broccoli
1 10-ounce container refrigerated Alfredo pasta sauce

6 ounces cooked smoked chicken or turkey breast, chopped
1 teaspoon dried basil, crushed
Grated Parmesan or Romano cheese (optional)

1

In a large saucepan bring 8 cups water to boiling. Add pasta and broccoli; cook for 3 minutes.

2

For sauce, in a medium saucepan combine the Alfredo sauce, chicken, and basil; cook over medium heat just until heated through (do not boil).

3

Drain pasta and broccoli; toss with sauce. If desired, serve with grated Parmesan or Romano cheese.

Nutrition Facts per serving: 501 calories, 24 g total fat, 126 mg cholesterol, 711 mg sodium, 49 g carbohydrate, 23 g protein.

CHICKEN-VEGETABLE RATATOUILLE

A medley of seasoned vegetables, typically including eggplant and tomatoes,
comprises the saucy mixture known as ratatouille.

Start to Finish: 30 minutes **Makes:** 4 or 5 servings

$2^2/_3$ cups dried penne (mostaccioli), cut
    ziti, or wagon wheel macaroni
    (ruote) (8 ounces)
1 cup chopped onion
1 teaspoon bottled minced garlic
1 tablespoon olive oil or cooking oil
1 medium eggplant, cut into 1-inch
    pieces
2 cups loose-pack frozen zucchini,
    carrots, cauliflower, lima beans,
    and Italian beans

1 $14^1/_2$-ounce can diced tomatoes
1 teaspoon dried Italian seasoning,
    crushed
$^3/_4$ teaspoon seasoned salt
$^1/_4$ teaspoon ground black pepper
$1^1/_2$ cups chopped cooked chicken
    (about 8 ounces)

1

In a large saucepan cook pasta according to package directions. Drain. Cover and keep warm.

2

Meanwhile, in a large saucepan cook onion and garlic in hot oil for 2 minutes. Stir in eggplant, frozen vegetables, undrained tomatoes, Italian seasoning, seasoned salt, and pepper. Bring to boiling; reduce heat. Cover and simmer for 12 to 15 minutes or until eggplant is tender.

3

Add chicken to vegetable mixture; cook about 1 minute more or until heated through. Serve chicken mixture over pasta.

Nutrition Facts per serving: 438 calories, 7 g total fat, 44 mg cholesterol, 651 mg sodium, 66 g carbohydrate, 28 g protein.

TURKEY-MAC CHILI

As the pasta simmers in the saucy turkey mixture, it absorbs the savory seasonings.

Prep: 15 minutes **Cook:** 17 minutes **Makes:** 4 servings

Nonstick cooking spray

8 ounces ground uncooked turkey or chicken

1 medium onion, chopped

2 cloves garlic, minced

1½ cups water

1 15-ounce can low-sodium tomato sauce

1 14½-ounce can low-sodium tomatoes, cut up

1 cup dried elbow macaroni or medium shell macaroni (about 4 ounces)

1 tablespoon chili powder

½ teaspoon dried basil, crushed

¼ teaspoon ground black pepper

⅛ teaspoon salt

1 15-ounce can reduced-sodium dark red kidney beans, rinsed and drained

Light dairy sour cream or plain low-fat yogurt (optional)

Ground red pepper (optional)

Fresh cilantro (optional)

1

Coat an unheated large saucepan with nonstick cooking spray. Preheat saucepan over medium heat. Add turkey or chicken, onion, and garlic; cook until turkey or chicken is no longer pink and onion is tender, stirring occasionally. Stir in the water, tomato sauce, undrained tomatoes, uncooked pasta, chili powder, basil, black pepper, and salt. Bring to boiling; reduce heat. Simmer, uncovered, for 17 to 20 minutes or until the pasta is tender and the mixture is of desired consistency. Stir in the beans; heat through.

2

To serve, ladle chili into bowls. If desired, top with sour cream or yogurt, sprinkle with ground red pepper, and garnish with cilantro.

Nutrition Facts per serving: 340 calories, 6 g total fat, 21 mg cholesterol, 304 mg sodium, 56 g carbohydrate, 21 g protein.

WHITE BEAN AND SAUSAGE RIGATONI

Preparing this dish on the stovetop, instead of baking it in the oven, allows you to make it in half of the time.

Start to Finish: 20 minutes **Makes:** 4 servings

8 ounces dried rigatoni

1 15-ounce can white kidney (cannellini), Great Northern, or navy beans, rinsed and drained

1 14$\frac{1}{2}$-ounce can Italian-style stewed tomatoes, undrained

6 ounces cooked smoked turkey sausage, cut into $\frac{1}{2}$-inch slices

$\frac{1}{3}$ cup snipped fresh basil

$\frac{1}{4}$ cup finely shredded Asiago or Parmesan cheese (1 ounce)

Shaved Asiago or Parmesan cheese (optional)

1

Cook pasta according to package directions, except omit any salt. Drain; return pasta to saucepan.

2

Meanwhile, in a large saucepan combine beans, undrained tomatoes, and sausage. Cook and stir until heated through. Add bean mixture and basil to cooked pasta; stir gently to combine. To serve, sprinkle each serving with shredded cheese. If desired, garnish with shaved cheese.

Nutrition Facts per serving: 401 calories, 6 g total fat, 32 mg cholesterol, 964 mg sodium, 67 g carbohydrate, 25 g protein.

FETTUCCINE AND SALMON

Poached salmon nestled on a bed of pasta and drizzled with a creamy sauce—now that's company special.

Start to Finish: 30 minutes **Makes:** 4 servings

1 1-pound fresh or frozen skinless
   salmon fillet, cut into 4 portions
   Nonstick cooking spray
$^1/_3$ cup finely chopped onion
$1^1/_2$ cups fat-free milk
$1^1/_2$ teaspoons cornstarch
6 ounces reduced-fat cream cheese
   (Neufchâtel), cubed and softened
$^1/_2$ cup finely shredded smoked Gouda
   cheese (2 ounces)
1 tablespoon snipped fresh chives

$^1/_4$ to $^1/_2$ teaspoon coarsely ground
   black pepper
$^1/_2$ of a 9-ounce package refrigerated
   linguine and $^1/_2$ of a 9-ounce
   package refrigerated spinach
   fettuccine or one 9-ounce package
   refrigerated linguine or spinach
   fettuccine
Fresh chives with blossoms
   (optional)

1

Thaw fish, if frozen. Rinse fish; pat dry. Measure thickness of fish. In a large skillet bring 2 cups water to boiling. Add fish to skillet. Return to boiling; reduce heat. Cover and simmer just until fish flakes easily with a fork. (Allow 4 to 6 minutes per $^1/_2$-inch thickness.) Drain. Cover and keep warm.

2

Meanwhile, for sauce, coat an unheated medium saucepan with nonstick cooking spray. Preheat over medium heat. Add onion and cook until tender. In a small bowl stir together milk and cornstarch. Add to saucepan. Cook and stir until slightly thickened and bubbly. Cook and stir for 2 minutes more. Add cream cheese and Gouda cheese; cook and stir until melted. Stir in snipped chives and black pepper.

3

Meanwhile, cook pasta according to package directions; drain. Divide hot pasta among 4 dinner plates. Place salmon on top of pasta. Spoon sauce over salmon. If desired, garnish with chives and blossoms.

Nutrition Facts per serving: 566 calories, 26 g total fat, 131 mg cholesterol, 579 mg sodium, 43 g carbohydrate, 40 g protein.

EASY SALMON PASTA

Cooking the pasta and vegetables together saves time and dishwashing.

Start to Finish: 25 minutes **Makes:** 5 servings

2 cups frozen loose-pack mixed
    vegetables or one 10-ounce
    package frozen mixed vegetables
$1^1/_2$ cups dried corkscrew macaroni
    (rotini) (about 4 ounces)
$^1/_4$ cup sliced green onions
1 $10^3/_4$-ounce can condensed cheddar
    cheese soup

$^1/_2$ cup milk
$^1/_2$ teaspoon dried dill
$^1/_4$ teaspoon dry mustard
$^1/_8$ teaspoon ground black pepper
2 6-ounce cans skinless, boneless
    salmon or tuna, drained
    Fresh dill sprigs (optional)

1

In a large saucepan cook frozen vegetables, pasta, and green onions in boiling water for 10 to 12 minutes or just until pasta is tender. Drain; return pasta and vegetables to saucepan.

2

Stir soup, milk, dried dill, mustard, and pepper into pasta mixture. Gently fold in salmon or tuna. Cook over low heat until heated through. If desired, garnish with fresh dill.

Nutrition Facts per serving: 347 calories, 9 g total fat, 56 mg cholesterol, 827 mg sodium, 41 g carbohydrate, 22 g protein.

PASTA WITH SMOKED SALMON AND LEMON CREAM

You'll be amazed that such an easy recipe can be so delicious and elegant.

Start to Finish: 20 minutes   **Makes:** 4 servings

8 ounces dried medium shell macaroni, cavatelli, or orecchiette
1 5-ounce container semisoft cheese with garlic and herbs
$1/3$ cup milk
1 teaspoon finely shredded lemon peel

1 tablespoon lemon juice
2 medium zucchini and/or yellow summer squash, halved lengthwise and thinly sliced (2 cups)
6 ounces thinly sliced, smoked salmon (lox-style), cut into $1/2$-inch strips
2 tablespoons snipped fresh chives

1
Cook pasta according to package directions. Drain; return pasta to saucepan.

2
Meanwhile, for sauce, in a medium saucepan heat the cheese and milk over low heat until cheese melts, whisking until smooth. Stir in lemon peel and lemon juice. Stir in squash and salmon; heat through. Pour sauce over cooked pasta. Toss to coat all ingredients.

3
Transfer to a warm serving platter. Sprinkle with chives.

Nutrition Facts per serving: 420 calories, 15 g total fat, 44 mg cholesterol, 347 mg sodium, 48 g carbohydrate, 19 g protein.

FETTUCCINE WITH HERBED SHRIMP

For best flavor and color, use ripe tomatoes from your garden or a farmer's market or purchase vine-ripened tomatoes at your supermarket.

Start to Finish: 25 minutes   **Makes:** 4 servings

12 ounces fresh or frozen peeled and deveined shrimp

6 ounces dried plain and/or spinach fettuccine or linguine

2 cups sliced fresh mushrooms

1 large onion, chopped

2 cloves garlic, minced

1 tablespoon olive oil or cooking oil

¼ cup dry white wine

1 tablespoon instant chicken bouillon granules

1 tablespoon snipped fresh basil or 1 teaspoon dried basil, crushed

1½ teaspoons snipped fresh oregano or ½ teaspoon dried oregano, crushed

1 teaspoon cornstarch

⅛ teaspoon ground black pepper

2 medium tomatoes, peeled, seeded, and chopped

¼ cup grated Parmesan cheese (1 ounce)

¼ cup snipped fresh parsley

1
Thaw shrimp, if frozen. Rinse shrimp; pat dry. Cut shrimp in half lengthwise. Set aside.

2
Cook pasta according to package directions. Drain. Cover and keep warm.

3
Meanwhile, in a large saucepan cook mushrooms, onion, and garlic in hot oil until onion is tender.

4
In a small bowl stir together wine, bouillon granules, basil, oregano, cornstarch, and pepper. Add to mushroom mixture. Cook and stir until thickened and bubbly.

5
Add shrimp to mushroom mixture. Cover and simmer about 2 minutes or until shrimp turn opaque. Stir in tomatoes; heat through.

6
Spoon the shrimp mixture over pasta. Sprinkle with Parmesan cheese and parsley. Toss to coat.

Nutrition Facts per serving: 351 calories, 7 g total fat, 136 mg cholesterol, 926 mg sodium, 44 g carbohydrate, 25 g protein.

LEMONY SCALLOPS AND SPAGHETTINI

Dinner is ready in a jiffy with this five-ingredient main dish.

Start to Finish: 20 minutes   **Makes:** 4 servings

12 ounces fresh or frozen scallops
8 ounces dried spaghettini (thin
   spaghetti) or spaghetti
3 cups small broccoli florets

1 10-ounce container refrigerated
   light Alfredo pasta sauce
1 teaspoon finely shredded lemon
   peel
   Lemon wedges (optional)

1

Thaw scallops, if frozen. Rinse scallops; pat dry. Cut any large scallops in half.

2

Cook pasta and broccoli according to pasta cooking directions about 6 minutes or just until broccoli is crisp-tender. Add scallops; cook for 1 to 2 minutes more or until scallops turn opaque. Drain well. Return to pan; stir in Alfredo sauce and lemon peel. Heat and stir about 2 minutes or until sauce is slightly thickened. If desired, garnish with lemon wedges.

Nutrition Facts per serving: 119 calories, 5 g total fat, 11 mg cholesterol, 759 mg sodium, 7 g carbohydrate, 14 g protein.

RAVIOLI WITH RED CLAM SAUCE

Round out the meal with a crisp green salad and crusty rolls.

Start to Finish: 25 minutes **Makes:** 3 servings

1 9-ounce package refrigerated
  cheese-filled ravioli or tortellini
1 14¹/₂-ounce can stewed tomatoes
1 6¹/₂-ounce can minced clams
1 medium zucchini, halved lengthwise
  and thinly sliced (1¹/₂ cups)

2 teaspoons dried Italian seasoning,
  crushed
1 8-ounce can tomato sauce
1 tablespoon cornstarch
  Grated Parmesan cheese

1

Cook ravioli or tortellini according to package directions. Drain. Cover and keep warm.

2

Meanwhile, in a medium saucepan combine stewed tomatoes, undrained clams, zucchini, and Italian seasoning. Bring to boiling; reduce heat. Simmer, uncovered, for 1 minute. In a small bowl stir together the tomato sauce and cornstarch; stir into hot mixture. Cook and stir over medium heat until thickened and bubbly. Cook and stir for 2 minutes more.

3

Serve clam sauce over hot pasta. Sprinkle with Parmesan cheese.

Nutrition Facts per serving: 406 calories, 16 g total fat, 113 mg cholesterol, 1,380 mg sodium, 46 g carbohydrate, 24 g protein.

LINGUINE WITH FENNEL AND SHRIMP IN ORANGE SAUCE

The delicate sauce gets its triple orange flavor from shredded orange peel, orange juice, and sliced oranges.

Start to Finish: 25 minutes **Makes:** 4 servings

8 ounces fresh or frozen peeled and deveined shrimp

8 ounces dried spinach, tomato-basil, or plain linguine or fettuccine

1 medium fennel bulb, trimmed and sliced (about 1½ cups)

1 tablespoon olive oil or cooking oil

1 cup chicken broth

1 tablespoon cornstarch

1 teaspoon finely shredded orange peel

¼ cup orange juice

2 oranges, peeled, halved lengthwise, and sliced

1 green onion, thinly sliced

Snipped fennel leaves

1

Thaw shrimp, if frozen. Rinse shrimp; pat dry. Set aside.

2

Cook pasta according to package directions until almost tender; add shrimp. Return to boiling; reduce heat. Simmer, uncovered, for 1 to 3 minutes more or until shrimp turn opaque and pasta is tender but still firm. Drain; return the pasta and shrimp to saucepan. Cover and keep warm.

3

Meanwhile, for sauce, in a medium saucepan cook sliced fennel in hot oil over medium heat for 3 to 5 minutes or until crisp-tender. In a small bowl stir together chicken broth and cornstarch; stir in orange peel and orange juice. Add broth mixture to saucepan. Cook and stir until thickened and bubbly. Cook and stir for 2 minutes more. Gently stir in orange slices.

4

Pour sauce over pasta mixture; toss gently to coat. Transfer to a warm serving dish. Sprinkle with green onion and snipped fennel leaves.

Nutrition Facts per serving: 342 calories, 5 g total fat, 87 mg cholesterol, 321 mg sodium, 54 g carbohydrate, 20 g protein.

CHILI-SAUCED PASTA

Dried linguine or fettuccine works equally well; it just takes a few more minutes to cook.

Start to Finish: 15 minutes **Makes:** 3 servings

6 ounces refrigerated linguine or
   fettuccine
1 14$\frac{1}{2}$-ounce can low-sodium stewed
   tomatoes
1 medium green sweet pepper, cut
   into thin bite-size strips
2 tablespoons low-sodium tomato
   paste

1 tablespoon chili powder
$\frac{1}{4}$ teaspoon salt
$\frac{1}{4}$ teaspoon garlic powder
$\frac{1}{4}$ teaspoon ground cumin
1 8-ounce can red kidney beans,
   rinsed and drained
$\frac{1}{4}$ cup cold water
2 teaspoons cornstarch

1

Cook pasta according to package directions, except omit any salt. Drain. Cover and keep warm.

2

Meanwhile, in a medium saucepan combine undrained stewed tomatoes, sweet pepper strips, tomato paste, chili powder, salt, garlic powder, and cumin. Bring to boiling; reduce heat. Cover and simmer for 3 minutes. Stir in kidney beans.

3

In a small bowl stir together the cold water and cornstarch; add to tomato mixture. Cook and stir until thickened and bubbly. Cook and stir for 2 minutes more. Serve tomato mixture over hot pasta.

Nutrition Facts per serving: 322 calories, 2 g total fat, 49 mg cholesterol, 392 mg sodium, 65 g carbohydrate, 15 g protein.

ROTINI AND SWEET PEPPER PRIMAVERA

Stop by the salad bar at your supermarket and pick up a cupful of sweet pepper chunks.

Start to Finish: 20 minutes   **Makes:** 4 servings

14 ounces fresh asparagus spears
8 ounces dried corkscrew macaroni
  (rotini) or rigatoni
1 cup mixed sweet pepper chunks
  from salad bar or 1 large red or
  yellow sweet pepper, cut into
  1-inch pieces
1 cup halved baby pattypan squash

1 10-ounce container refrigerated
  light Alfredo pasta sauce
2 tablespoons snipped fresh tarragon
  or thyme
$1/4$ teaspoon crushed red pepper
  Coarsely ground black pepper
  (optional)

1

Snap off and discard woody bases from asparagus. Bias-slice asparagus into 1-inch pieces (you should have about $1^1/_2$ cups).

2

Cook pasta according to package directions, adding asparagus, sweet pepper, and squash to pasta for the last 3 minutes of cooking. Drain; return pasta and vegetables to saucepan. Cover and keep warm.

3

Meanwhile, in a small saucepan combine Alfredo sauce, tarragon or thyme, and crushed red pepper. Cook and stir over medium heat about 5 minutes or until heated through. Pour over pasta and vegetables; toss gently to coat. If desired, sprinkle with black pepper.

Nutrition Facts per serving: 421 calories, 12 g total fat, 31 mg cholesterol, 622 mg sodium, 66 g carbohydrate, 15 g protein.

TORTELLINI ALFREDO WITH ROASTED PEPPERS

To shred the basil quickly, pile several leaves on top of each other, roll up the leaves, and slice crosswise to make shreds.

Start to Finish: 20 minutes **Makes:** 3 servings

1 9-ounce package refrigerated meat- or cheese-filled tortellini or ravioli

½ cup refrigerated light Alfredo pasta sauce

½ of a 7-ounce jar roasted red sweet peppers, drained and cut into ½-inch-wide strips

½ cup shredded fresh basil

¼ to ½ teaspoon coarsely ground black pepper

1

Cook pasta according to package directions. Drain. Cover and keep warm.

2

In a large saucepan heat Alfredo sauce. Stir in cooked and drained tortellini or ravioli; reduce heat. Stir in roasted sweet peppers; heat through. Stir in half of the basil.

3

To serve, top with remaining basil and black pepper.

Nutrition Facts per serving: 362 calories, 12 g total fat, 61 mg cholesterol, 710 mg sodium, 50 g carbohydrate, 16 g protein.

FETTUCCINE ALLA CARBONARA

This revamped classic uses egg product (which is pasteurized) rather than the traditional raw eggs.

Start to Finish: 20 minutes **Makes:** 4 servings

1/4 cup refrigerated or frozen egg
   product, thawed
2 tablespoons evaporated fat-free
   milk or fat-free milk
4 ounces dried fettuccine or linguine

2 teaspoons margarine or butter
1/4 cup grated Parmesan cheese
   (1 ounce)
2 tablespoons snipped fresh parsley
1 tablespoon cooked bacon pieces

1

In a small bowl stir together the egg product and milk. Set aside.

2

In a large saucepan cook the fettuccine or linguine according to package directions, except omit any oil
or salt. Drain well.

3

Return pasta to the hot saucepan. Immediately pour the egg product mixture over pasta. Add
margarine or butter. Heat and stir over low heat about 2 minutes or until mixture thickens and pasta is
well coated. Add the Parmesan cheese, parsley, and cooked bacon pieces; toss until combined.
Serve immediately.

Nutrition Facts per serving: 195 calories, 6 g total fat, 6 mg cholesterol, 184 mg sodium, 25 g carbohydrate, 9 g protein.

TORTELLINI WITH CREAMY VEGETABLES

Neufchâtel cheese and evaporated fat-free milk add richness, but not much fat, to the creamy sauce.

Start to Finish: 25 minutes **Makes:** 4 servings

1 9-ounce package refrigerated cheese-filled tortellini or ravioli

1 9-ounce package frozen artichoke hearts

1/2 of a 6-ounce package frozen pea pods (about 1 cup)

1 7-ounce jar roasted red sweet peppers, drained and cut into thin strips

1/2 of an 8-ounce package reduced-fat cream cheese (Neufchâtel), cut up

1 cup evaporated fat-free milk

1/8 teaspoon salt

1/8 teaspoon ground black pepper
   Fresh herb sprigs (optional)

1/4 cup grated Parmesan cheese (1 ounce)

1

Bring a large amount of water to boiling in a 4-quart Dutch oven. Add tortellini or ravioli and artichoke hearts. Return to boiling; reduce heat. Simmer, uncovered, for 6 minutes. Add pea pods; cook for 1 minute more or until pasta and vegetables are tender. Drain. Stir in red pepper strips. Cover and keep warm.

2

Meanwhile, in a medium saucepan combine cream cheese, evaporated milk, salt, and black pepper. Cook and stir over medium heat until slightly thickened and smooth. Pour over pasta mixture. Sprinkle with 2 tablespoons of the Parmesan cheese; toss gently. If desired, garnish with fresh herb sprigs. Sprinkle with remaining Parmesan cheese just before serving.

Nutrition Facts per serving: 408 calories, 14 g total fat, 59 mg cholesterol, 684 mg sodium, 51 g carbohydrate, 24 g protein.

EASY OVEN DISHES

These baked pastas will fill your kitchen with such superb aromas, you'll hardly be able to wait for dinner.

Bow Ties and Cheese
(see recipe, page 138)

SAUCY SPICED SHELLS

The spices make the ground meat mixture for these generously-filled shells taste like sausage.

Prep: 25 minutes **Bake:** 25 minutes **Makes:** 4 servings

- 12 **dried jumbo shell macaroni (conchiglioni)**
- 12 **ounces ground beef, pork, or lamb**
- 1/2 **cup chopped onion**
- 1/2 **cup chopped green sweet pepper**
- 1 **clove garlic, minced**
- 1 **beaten egg**
- 1/4 **cup fine dry bread crumbs**

- 1/4 **teaspoon ground cinnamon**
- 1/4 **teaspoon ground allspice**
- 1/4 **teaspoon ground black pepper**
- 1 **15-ounce container refrigerated marinara sauce or one 14-ounce jar meatless spaghetti sauce**
- **Shredded or grated Parmesan cheese (optional)**

1

Cook pasta according to package directions. Drain. Rinse pasta with cold water; drain again.

2

Meanwhile, in a large skillet cook ground meat, onion, sweet pepper, and garlic until meat is browned. Drain off fat.

3

In a medium bowl combine egg, bread crumbs, cinnamon, allspice, and black pepper. Add the meat mixture and 1/4 cup of the sauce; mix well. Spoon about 2 tablespoons of the meat mixture into each cooked shell. Arrange the filled shells in a 2-quart square baking dish. Pour the remaining sauce over the filled shells. Cover the dish with foil.

4

Bake in a 375°F oven for 25 to 30 minutes or until heated through. For each serving, arrange 3 of the shells on a dinner plate. Spoon some of the sauce over the shells. If desired, sprinkle each serving with Parmesan cheese.

Nutrition Facts per serving: 325 calories, 12 g total fat, 107 mg cholesterol, 445 mg sodium, 30 g carbohydrate, 23 g protein.

BAKED RAVIOLI WITH MEAT SAUCE

To make individual servings use six 10-ounce casseroles in place of the 2-quart square baking dish. Cover and bake for 25 to 30 minutes.

Prep: 25 minutes **Bake:** 45 minutes **Makes:** 6 servings

8 ounces ground beef, ground pork, or bulk pork sausage
$\frac{1}{2}$ cup finely chopped carrot
$\frac{1}{3}$ cup chopped onion
1 clove garlic, minced
1 14$\frac{1}{2}$-ounce can diced tomatoes
1 cup water*
1 6-ounce can tomato paste
$\frac{1}{2}$ cup diced cooked ham or crumbled, crisp-cooked bacon

2 teaspoons sugar
2 teaspoons dried Italian seasoning, crushed
$\frac{1}{4}$ teaspoon ground black pepper
$\frac{1}{2}$ of a 25-ounce package frozen cheese-filled ravioli or one 16-ounce package frozen cheese-filled tortellini
1 cup shredded mozzarella cheese (4 ounces)

1

For meat sauce, in a large skillet cook ground meat or sausage, carrot, onion, and garlic until meat is browned and onion is tender. Drain off fat.

2

Stir in undrained tomatoes, the water, tomato paste, ham or bacon, sugar, Italian seasoning, and pepper. Bring to boiling; reduce heat. Simmer for 5 minutes, stirring occasionally.

3

Spoon one-third of the meat sauce into a 2-quart square baking dish. Arrange frozen ravioli or tortellini on top of the meat sauce. Sprinkle with $\frac{1}{2}$ cup of the mozzarella cheese. Top with the remaining meat sauce.

4

Cover and bake in a 350°F oven for 40 to 45 minutes or until pasta is tender. Uncover and sprinkle with remaining mozzarella cheese. Bake about 5 minutes more or until cheese melts.

Nutrition Facts per serving: 401 calories, 17 g total fat, 98 mg cholesterol, 666 mg sodium, 37 g carbohydrate, 26 g protein.

*Note: If desired, reduce the water to $\frac{3}{4}$ cup and add $\frac{1}{4}$ cup dry red wine.

BAKED CAVATELLI

Vary the hotness of this dish by the type of sausage you use. If you love spicy foods, try hot Italian sausage. If not, opt for the mild or sweet version.

Prep: 25 minutes **Bake:** 30 minutes **Makes:** 6 servings

- 2¹/₂ cups dried cavatelli or wagon wheel macaroni (about 7 ounces)
- 12 ounces fresh Italian sausage links, cut into ¹/₂-inch-thick slices
- ³/₄ cup chopped onion
- 2 cloves garlic, minced
- 1 15-ounce can tomato sauce

- 1 14-ounce jar spaghetti sauce with mushrooms
- 1 cup shredded mozzarella cheese (4 ounces)
- 1 teaspoon dried Italian seasoning, crushed
- ¹/₄ teaspoon ground black pepper

1
Cook pasta according to package directions. Drain.

2
Meanwhile, in a large skillet cook the sausage, onion, and garlic until sausage is browned; remove from skillet. Drain off fat.

3
In a large bowl stir together the tomato sauce, spaghetti sauce, ¹/₂ cup of the mozzarella cheese, the Italian seasoning, and pepper. Add the cooked pasta and the sausage mixture. Toss gently to combine. Spoon the mixture into a 2-quart casserole.*

4
Cover and bake in a 375°F oven for 25 minutes. Uncover and sprinkle with the remaining ¹/₂ cup mozzarella cheese. Bake for 5 to 10 minutes more or until heated through.

Nutrition Facts per serving: 418 calories, 17 g total fat, 50 mg cholesterol, 1,268 mg sodium, 46 g carbohydrate, 20 g protein.

*Note: To serve individual portions, spoon the mixture into six 10-ounce casseroles. Place the casseroles on a large baking sheet. Cover the casseroles with foil and bake for 15 minutes. Uncover, sprinkle with remaining cheese, and bake for 5 to 10 minutes more or until heated through.

HAM, SPINACH, AND MOSTACCIOLI CASSEROLE

All you need to round out this one-dish meal is some French bread or breadsticks.

Prep: 20 minutes **Bake:** 30 minutes **Stand:** 5 minutes **Makes:** 6 servings

8 ounces dried penne (mostaccioli), cut ziti, or elbow macaroni
3 tablespoons margarine or butter
3 medium onions, cut into thin wedges, or 5 medium leeks, sliced
2 cloves garlic, minced
1/4 cup all-purpose flour
1/2 teaspoon dried thyme, crushed
1/8 teaspoon ground black pepper
1 1/2 cups half-and-half, light cream, or milk
1 1/2 cups chicken broth
1 1/2 cups cubed cooked ham
1 10-ounce package frozen chopped spinach, thawed and drained

1

Cook pasta according to package directions. Drain. Rinse pasta with cold water; drain again.

2

Meanwhile, in a large saucepan melt margarine or butter. Add onions or leeks and garlic. Cover and cook about 5 minutes or until onions are tender, stirring occasionally. Stir in flour, thyme, and pepper. Add half-and-half, light cream, or milk and the chicken broth all at once. Cook and stir until thickened and bubbly. Cook and stir for 1 minute more. Stir in cooked pasta, ham, and spinach. Spoon mixture into a 3-quart casserole.

3

Cover and bake in a 350°F oven for 30 to 35 minutes or until heated through. Let stand for 5 minutes. Stir gently before serving.

Nutrition Facts per serving: 328 calories, 16 g total fat, 42 mg cholesterol, 719 mg sodium, 44 g carbohydrate, 18 g protein.

CHICKEN AND PROSCIUTTO PASTA

Look for proscuitto—a salt-cured ham—in Italian specialty markets or larger supermarkets.

Prep: 30 minutes **Bake:** 25 minutes **Makes:** 6 servings

Nonstick cooking spray
6 ounces dried penne (mostaccioli) (about 2 cups)
1 tablespoon olive oil
12 ounces skinless, boneless chicken breast halves, cut into $1/2$-inch-wide strips
2 cloves garlic, minced
4 ounces sliced prosciutto or ham, coarsely chopped
$1/2$ of a medium green sweet pepper, cut into thin bite-size strips

$1/2$ of a medium yellow sweet pepper, cut into thin bite-size strips
1 teaspoon dried basil, crushed
1 tablespoon drained capers (optional)
1 15-ounce container refrigerated marinara sauce
1 10-ounce container refrigerated Alfredo sauce
$1/3$ cup finely shredded Parmesan cheese
Fresh basil sprig (optional)

1
Coat a 2-quart casserole with nonstick cooking spray; set aside. Cook pasta according to package directions. Drain; return pasta to saucepan.

2
Meanwhile, in large skillet heat oil over medium-high heat. Add chicken and garlic; cook and stir for 2 minutes. Add prosciutto or ham, green sweet pepper, yellow sweet pepper, dried basil, and, if desired, capers. Cook and stir 2 to 3 minutes longer or until chicken is no longer pink and peppers are crisp-tender. Add to pasta in saucepan; mix well.

3
Layer half of the pasta mixture in the prepared casserole. Top with 1 cup of the marinara sauce. Top with the remaining pasta mixture; then add the remaining marinara sauce. Drizzle with Alfredo sauce. Sprinkle with Parmesan cheese.

4
Bake, uncovered, in a 350°F oven for 25 to 35 minutes or until heated through. If desired, garnish with a sprig of fresh basil.

Nutrition Facts per serving: 465 calories, 26 g total fat, 62 mg cholesterol, 839 mg sodium, 30 g carbohydrate, 28 g protein.

SPICY PASTA PIE

Thinner than spaghetti but thicker than angel hair pasta, vermicelli makes an ideal partner for this zesty turkey sausage-and-mushroom filling.

Prep: 25 minutes **Bake:** 25 minutes **Stand:** 10 minutes **Makes:** 6 servings

4 ounces dried vermicelli, broken
1 beaten egg white
   Nonstick cooking spray
1 cup shredded mozzarella cheese
   (4 ounces)
1 pound turkey breakfast sausage
1 cup sliced fresh mushrooms
1/2 cup chopped onion
1 clove garlic, minced

1 7 1/2-ounce can low-sodium
   tomatoes, undrained and cut up
1/2 of a 6-ounce can (1/3 cup) tomato
   paste
1 teaspoon dried Italian seasoning,
   crushed
1/8 teaspoon crushed red pepper
2 tablespoons grated Parmesan or
   Romano cheese
   Celery leaves (optional)

1

Cook vermicelli according to package directions, except omit any oil and salt. Drain. Toss with the egg white. Coat a 9-inch quiche dish or pie plate with nonstick cooking spray. Press vermicelli mixture into bottom of prepared dish. Sprinkle with mozzarella cheese. Set aside.

2

Meanwhile, in a large skillet cook the turkey sausage, mushrooms, onion, and garlic until sausage is browned and onion is tender. Drain off fat. Stir in the undrained tomatoes, tomato paste, Italian seasoning, and crushed red pepper. Pour sausage mixture over cheese layer.

3

Cover dish loosely with foil. Bake in a 350°F oven for 25 to 30 minutes or until heated through. Uncover; sprinkle with the Parmesan or Romano cheese. Let stand for 10 minute before serving. If desired, garnish with the celery leaves.

Nutrition Facts per serving: 316 calories, 14 g total fat, 41 mg cholesterol, 732 mg sodium, 22 g carbohydrate, 26 g protein.

TURKEY-AND-BROCCOLI-FILLED LASAGNA ROLLS

These tender lasagna noodle spirals are brimming with a sassy turkey, broccoli, and ricotta cheese filling. For a special presentation, used shaved Parmesan cheese in place of shredded.

Prep: 30 minutes **Bake:** 30 minutes **Makes:** 4 servings

4 dried lasagna noodles

6 ounces uncooked ground turkey or chicken

1/4 cup chopped onion

1 cup chopped fresh broccoli

1/4 cup water

1 beaten egg

1 cup ricotta cheese or cream-style cottage cheese, drained

1 1/2 teaspoons snipped fresh thyme or 1/2 teaspoon dried thyme, crushed

1 1/2 cups meatless spaghetti sauce

1/4 cup finely shaved Parmesan cheese

1

Cook lasagna noodles according to package directions. Drain. Rinse noodles with cold water; drain again.

2

Meanwhile, for filling, in a large skillet cook ground turkey or chicken and onion until turkey is browned and onion is tender. Drain off fat. Stir in broccoli and the water. Bring to boiling; reduce heat. Cover and simmer about 5 minutes or until broccoli is crisp-tender. Drain.

3

In a bowl stir together egg, ricotta or cottage cheese, and thyme; stir in turkey mixture. Divide filling mixture into 4 equal portions. Spread 1 portion over each lasagna noodle; roll up each noodle into a spiral. Place rolls, seam sides down, in a 2-quart square baking dish. Spoon spaghetti sauce over rolls.

4

Cover and bake in a 375°F oven about 30 minutes or until heated through. Uncover and top with the Parmesan cheese.

Nutrition Facts per serving: 383 calories, 16 g total fat, 93 mg cholesterol, 666 mg sodium, 38 g carbohydrate, 23 g protein.

SPINACH AND ORZO PIE

Rice-shaped orzo pasta mixed with egg, Parmesan cheese, and spaghetti sauce bakes up into a sturdy crust to hold the spinach-and-ricotta cheese filling.

Prep: 25 minutes **Bake:** 33 minutes **Stand:** 5 minutes **Makes:** 6 servings

1$\frac{1}{2}$ cups dried orzo (rosamarina) (about 9 ounces)
1 10-ounce package frozen chopped spinach
2 beaten eggs
1 14-ounce jar chunky spaghetti sauce

$\frac{1}{3}$ cup grated Parmesan cheese
$\frac{1}{2}$ cup ricotta cheese
$\frac{1}{4}$ teaspoon ground nutmeg
$\frac{1}{2}$ cup shredded fontina or mozzarella cheese (2 ounces)

1

Cook pasta according to package directions. Drain. Rinse pasta with cold water; drain again. Cook spinach according to package directions. Drain well.

2

Meanwhile, grease a 9-inch pie plate. Set aside. In a medium bowl combine eggs, $\frac{1}{2}$ cup of the spaghetti sauce, and the Parmesan cheese. Add cooked pasta; toss to coat. Spread pasta mixture over the bottom and up the side of prepared pie plate to form an even shell.

3

In another bowl stir together cooked spinach, ricotta cheese, and nutmeg. Spoon into pasta-lined pie plate. Spread remaining spaghetti sauce over spinach mixture. Cover edge of pie with foil.

4

Bake, uncovered, in a 350°F oven for 30 minutes. Sprinkle with fontina or mozzarella cheese. Bake for 3 to 5 minutes more or until cheese melts. Let stand for 5 minutes before serving.

Nutrition Facts per serving: 374 calories, 12 g total fat, 93 mg cholesterol, 617 mg sodium, 49 g carbohydrate, 17 g protein.

NEW MILLENNIUM MACARONI AND CHEESE

This newfangled take on an old favorite is loaded with flavor and protein.

Prep: 25 minutes **Bake:** 55 minutes **Makes:** 5 servings

1½ cups dried whole wheat elbow
    macaroni (about 6 ounces)
8 ounces light tofu, cut up
    (about 1⅓ cups)
½ of a 7-ounce jar roasted red sweet
    peppers, drained (about ½ cup)
4 or 5 large cloves garlic, cut up
¼ cup fat-free milk
1 tablespoon red wine vinegar
2 teaspoons soy sauce or
    Worcestershire sauce

1 teaspoon olive oil
¼ teaspoon habañero sauce or bottled
    hot pepper sauce
1½ cups shredded sharp cheddar cheese
    or reduced-fat sharp cheddar
    cheese (6 ounces)
¾ cup reduced-fat or fat-free dairy
    sour cream
1 medium tomato, cut into wedges
2 tablespoons snipped fresh parsley

1

Cook pasta according to package directions. Drain.

2

Meanwhile, in a blender container or food processor bowl combine tofu, roasted peppers, garlic, milk, vinegar, soy sauce or Worcestershire sauce, oil, and the habañero sauce or pepper sauce. Cover and blend or process until smooth, stopping to scrape sides of blender or food processor bowl as necessary. Transfer sauce to a large bowl. Stir in cooked pasta, cheese, and sour cream. Spoon pasta mixture to a 2-quart casserole.

3

Cover and bake in 350°F oven for 30 minutes. Uncover and bake 25 minutes more or until lightly browned and bubbly. Remove from oven and garnish top of casserole with tomato and parsley.

Nutrition Facts per serving: 350 calories, 16 g total fat, 48 mg cholesterol, 409 mg sodium, 33 g carbohydrate, 20 g protein.

BOW TIES AND CHEESE

Macaroni and cheese gets a delectable makeover with this easy recipe. Serve it with your favorite steamed vegetable. (Pictured on page 121.)

Prep: 20 minutes **Bake:** 30 minutes **Makes:** 5 servings

8 ounces dried large bow ties (farfalle)
$1/4$ cup finely chopped onion
2 teaspoons cooking oil
2 teaspoons all-purpose flour
1 teaspoon dry mustard
$1/3$ cup fat-free milk
1 cup fat-free cottage cheese

$2/3$ cup shredded reduced-fat cheddar cheese
Nonstick cooking spray
1 tablespoon toasted wheat germ or fine dry bread crumbs
Chopped tomato (optional)
Sliced green onion (optional)

1

Cook pasta according to package directions, except omit any oil. Drain.

2

Meanwhile, in a large saucepan cook chopped onion in hot oil until tender. Stir in the flour and mustard. Add milk all at once. Cook and stir until thickened and bubbly. Stir in the cottage cheese and cheddar cheese. Cook and stir over low heat until cheddar cheese is melted. Stir in the cooked pasta.

3

Coat a $1^{1}/_{2}$-quart casserole with nonstick cooking spray. Spoon pasta mixture into casserole. Cover and bake in a 350°F oven for 20 minutes. Uncover and sprinkle with wheat germ or bread crumbs. Bake, uncovered, for 10 to 15 minutes more or until heated through. If desired, garnish with tomato and green onion.

Nutrition Facts per serving: 296 calories, 6 g total fat, 16 mg cholesterol, 301 mg sodium, 40 g carbohydrate, 19 g protein.

SPINACH LASAGNA

Don't skimp on the standing time. It allows the lasagna to set up so that it's easier to serve.

Prep: 25 minutes **Bake:** 30 minutes **Stand:** 10 minutes **Makes:** 8 servings

9 dried lasagna noodles
1 cup chopped onion
1 cup sliced fresh mushrooms
4 cloves garlic, minced
2 tablespoons margarine or butter
1 7-ounce jar roasted red sweet
  peppers, drained and chopped
1 10-ounce package frozen chopped
  spinach, thawed and well drained
1 15-ounce container ricotta cheese
1 cup shredded mozzarella cheese
  (4 ounces)

$1/2$ cup grated Parmesan or Romano
  cheese (2 ounces)
2 beaten eggs
1 teaspoon dried basil, crushed
$1/2$ teaspoon dried oregano, crushed
$1/4$ teaspoon ground black pepper
1 26- or 28-ounce jar meatless
  spaghetti sauce
$1/4$ cup grated Parmesan or Romano
  cheese

1

Cook lasagna noodles according to package directions. Drain. Rinse noodles with cold water; drain again.

2

Meanwhile, in a large skillet cook onion, mushrooms, and garlic in hot margarine or butter until tender. Stir in roasted peppers. Set aside.

3

Pat spinach dry with paper towels. In a medium bowl stir together spinach, ricotta cheese, mozzarella cheese, the $1/2$ cup Parmesan or Romano cheese, the eggs, basil, oregano, and black pepper. Stir roasted pepper mixture into spinach mixture.

4

Spread $1/2$ cup of the spaghetti sauce evenly in a 3-quart rectangular baking dish. Arrange 3 lasagna noodles over sauce. Layer with half the sweet pepper-spinach mixture and 1 cup of the spaghetti sauce. Add another layer of noodles and the remaining sweet pepper-spinach mixture. Top with 1 cup of the spaghetti sauce. End with the remaining noodles and remaining spaghetti sauce. Sprinkle with the $1/4$ cup Parmesan or Romano cheese.

5

Cover and bake in a 375°F oven for 20 minutes. Uncover and bake about 10 minutes more or until heated through. Let stand for 10 minutes before serving.

Nutrition Facts per serving: 455 calories, 19 g total fat, 105 mg cholesterol, 980 mg sodium, 50 g carbohydrate, 22 g protein.

SOUPS

These homey meals-in-a-bowl are loaded with pasta and so scrumptious you'll spoon up every last drop.

Fish and Shell Stew
(see recipe, page 156)

BEEF-VEGETABLE STEW WITH PASTA

Stew in just 30 minutes—sound impossible? Using quick-cooking beef tenderloin is the key.

Start to Finish: 30 minutes **Makes:** 4 servings

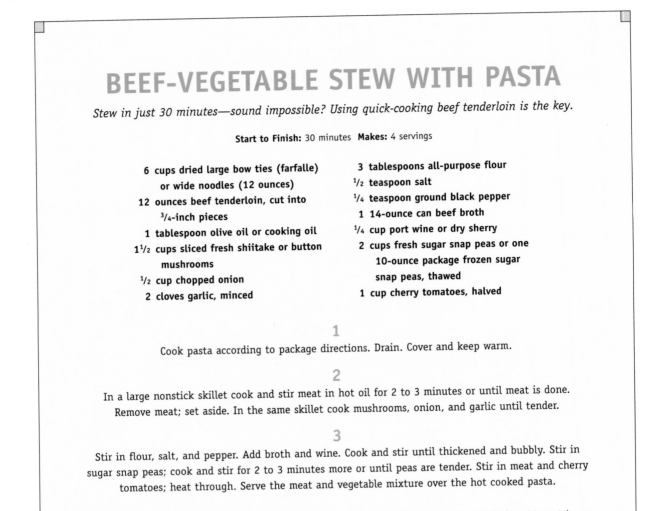

6 cups dried large bow ties (farfalle) or wide noodles (12 ounces)

12 ounces beef tenderloin, cut into ³/₄-inch pieces

1 tablespoon olive oil or cooking oil

1¹/₂ cups sliced fresh shiitake or button mushrooms

¹/₂ cup chopped onion

2 cloves garlic, minced

3 tablespoons all-purpose flour

¹/₂ teaspoon salt

¹/₄ teaspoon ground black pepper

1 14-ounce can beef broth

¹/₄ cup port wine or dry sherry

2 cups fresh sugar snap peas or one 10-ounce package frozen sugar snap peas, thawed

1 cup cherry tomatoes, halved

1

Cook pasta according to package directions. Drain. Cover and keep warm.

2

In a large nonstick skillet cook and stir meat in hot oil for 2 to 3 minutes or until meat is done. Remove meat; set aside. In the same skillet cook mushrooms, onion, and garlic until tender.

3

Stir in flour, salt, and pepper. Add broth and wine. Cook and stir until thickened and bubbly. Stir in sugar snap peas; cook and stir for 2 to 3 minutes more or until peas are tender. Stir in meat and cherry tomatoes; heat through. Serve the meat and vegetable mixture over the hot cooked pasta.

Nutrition Facts per serving: 620 calories, 14 g total fat, 133 mg cholesterol, 620 mg sodium, 82 g carbohydrate, 37 g protein.

HAM, PASTA, AND BEAN SOUP

Perk up the soup's color by using tricolor wagon wheel macaroni.

Prep: 20 minutes **Cook:** 10 minutes **Makes:** 4 servings

1 15-ounce can navy beans, rinsed
   and drained
2¹/₂ cups water
2 cups chicken broth
¹/₂ teaspoon dried marjoram or basil,
   crushed
¹/₄ teaspoon ground black pepper

1 cup dried tricolor wagon wheel
   macaroni (ruote) or elbow
   macaroni (about 3 ounces)
1 cup cubed cooked ham or cooked
   smoked turkey (about 5 ounces)
1 medium onion, chopped
1 stalk celery, sliced

1

Using a potato masher or fork, mash about half of the navy beans. Set whole and
mashed navy beans aside.

2

In a large saucepan combine the water, chicken broth, marjoram or basil, and pepper. Bring to boiling.
Add the mashed and whole navy beans, macaroni, ham or smoked turkey, onion, and celery to the
broth mixture. Return to boiling; reduce heat. Simmer, uncovered, for 10 to 15 minutes or until
macaroni is tender but still slightly firm, stirring occasionally.

Nutrition Facts per serving: 275 calories, 3 g total fat, 11 mg cholesterol, 1,090 mg sodium, 40 g carbohydrate, 21 g protein.

ASIAN CHICKEN NOODLE SOUP

The addition of soy sauce, fresh ginger, and pea pods gives the all-American classic soup an Asian flair.

Start to Finish: 20 minutes   **Makes:** 3 servings

2 14-ounce cans chicken broth
1 cup water
3/4 cup dried fine egg noodles or broken angel hair pasta (capellini) (about 1 1/2 ounces)
1 tablespoon soy sauce
1 teaspoon grated fresh ginger
1/8 teaspoon crushed red pepper
1 medium red sweet pepper, cut into 3/4-inch pieces

1 medium carrot, chopped
1/3 cup thinly sliced green onions
1 cup chopped cooked chicken or turkey (about 5 ounces)
1 cup fresh pea pods, halved crosswise, or 1/2 of a 6-ounce package frozen pea pods, thawed and halved crosswise

1

In a large saucepan combine chicken broth, the water, noodles or pasta, soy sauce, ginger, and crushed red pepper. Bring to boiling. Stir in sweet pepper, carrot, and green onions. Return to boiling; reduce heat. Cover and simmer for 4 to 6 minutes or until vegetables are crisp-tender and noodles are tender.

2

Stir in chicken or turkey and pea pods. Simmer, uncovered, for 1 to 2 minutes more or until pea pods are crisp-tender.

Nutrition Facts per serving: 224 calories, 6 g total fat, 58 mg cholesterol, 1,280 mg sodium, 17 g carbohydrate, 24 g protein.

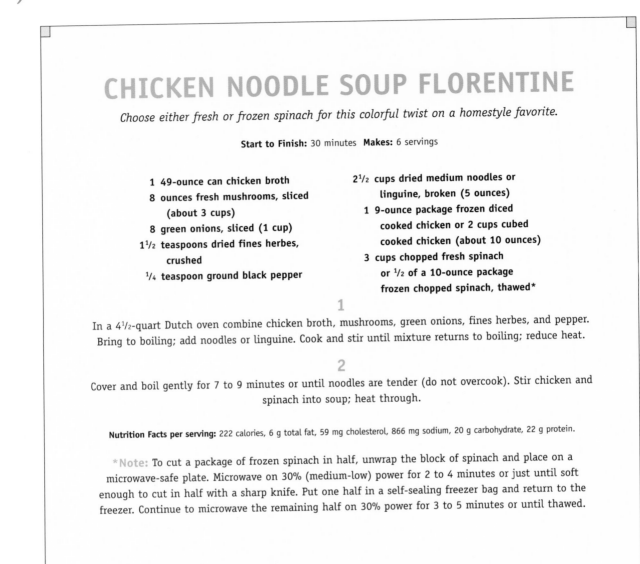

CHICKEN NOODLE SOUP FLORENTINE

Choose either fresh or frozen spinach for this colorful twist on a homestyle favorite.

Start to Finish: 30 minutes **Makes:** 6 servings

1 49-ounce can chicken broth
8 ounces fresh mushrooms, sliced
   (about 3 cups)
8 green onions, sliced (1 cup)
1½ teaspoons dried fines herbes,
   crushed
¼ teaspoon ground black pepper

2½ cups dried medium noodles or
   linguine, broken (5 ounces)
1 9-ounce package frozen diced
   cooked chicken or 2 cups cubed
   cooked chicken (about 10 ounces)
3 cups chopped fresh spinach
   or ½ of a 10-ounce package
   frozen chopped spinach, thawed*

1

In a 4½-quart Dutch oven combine chicken broth, mushrooms, green onions, fines herbes, and pepper. Bring to boiling; add noodles or linguine. Cook and stir until mixture returns to boiling; reduce heat.

2

Cover and boil gently for 7 to 9 minutes or until noodles are tender (do not overcook). Stir chicken and spinach into soup; heat through.

Nutrition Facts per serving: 222 calories, 6 g total fat, 59 mg cholesterol, 866 mg sodium, 20 g carbohydrate, 22 g protein.

*Note: To cut a package of frozen spinach in half, unwrap the block of spinach and place on a microwave-safe plate. Microwave on 30% (medium-low) power for 2 to 4 minutes or just until soft enough to cut in half with a sharp knife. Put one half in a self-sealing freezer bag and return to the freezer. Continue to microwave the remaining half on 30% power for 3 to 5 minutes or until thawed.

SOUP WITH MIXED PASTAS

Raid your pantry for a little bit of two or three kinds of pasta. Using a combination of shapes adds interest to this easy-fixing soup.

Start to Finish: 30 minutes **Makes:** 3 servings

4 cups reduced-sodium chicken broth
1 cup water
3 bay leaves
1 large onion, chopped
1 large carrot, chopped
4 cloves garlic, minced
4 ounces skinless, boneless chicken breasts, coarsely chopped
1 teaspoon olive oil or cooking oil

1 to 1½ cups assorted dried small pastas (such as tiny bow ties [tripolini], corkscrew macaroni [rotini], ditalini, wagon wheel macaroni [ruote], shell macaroni, and/or broken spaghetti) (2 to 3 ounces)
Snipped fresh sage*

1

In a large saucepan bring chicken broth and the water to boiling. Add bay leaves, onion, carrot, and garlic. Reduce heat. Simmer, uncovered, for 10 minutes.

2

In a medium skillet cook chicken in hot oil over medium-high heat about 2 minutes or until browned.

3

Add chicken, desired pasta, and desired amount of sage to saucepan. Simmer, uncovered, for 8 to 10 minutes or until the larger pieces of pasta are tender but still firm. Discard bay leaves.

Nutrition Facts per serving: 220 calories, 6 g total fat, 20 mg cholesterol, 896 mg sodium, 28 g carbohydrate, 14 g protein.

*Note: Season the soup with enough snipped fresh sage to suit your taste. Start with about 1 teaspoon and add additional as desired.

TUSCAN RAVIOLI STEW

Chop the leaves, stalks, and buds of thin-stalked broccoli rabe (also known as rapini) for this hearty stew. If you can't find broccoli rabe, substitute 5 cups coarsely chopped escarole or broccoli buds and add to the stew for the last 2 to 3 minutes of cooking.

Start to Finish: 35 minutes **Makes:** 4 servings

1 large leek, thinly sliced (white and light green parts only) (about 1½ cups)

3 cloves garlic, minced

1 tablespoon olive oil

1 14-ounce can beef or chicken broth

¾ cup water, beef broth, or chicken broth

¼ teaspoon crushed red pepper (optional)

1 9-ounce package refrigerated chicken- or cheese-filled ravioli

6 ounces broccoli rabe, coarsely chopped (5 cups)

1 14½-ounce can low-sodium stewed tomatoes

1 tablespoon snipped fresh rosemary or 1 teaspoon dried rosemary, crushed

¼ cup shredded Asiago or Romano cheese (1 ounce)

1

In a large saucepan cook leek and garlic in hot oil over medium heat for 5 minutes, stirring occasionally. Add the 14-ounce can broth, the ¾ cup water or additional broth, and, if desired, the crushed red pepper. Bring to boiling.

2

Stir in ravioli, broccoli rabe, undrained tomatoes, and rosemary. Return to boiling; reduce heat. Cover and simmer for 7 to 8 minutes or until ravioli and broccoli rabe are tender. Ladle into shallow bowls; top with cheese.

Nutrition Facts per serving: 320 calories, 13 g total fat, 65 mg cholesterol, 704 mg sodium, 38 g carbohydrate, 15 g protein.

CRAB AND PASTA GAZPACHO

For a simple yet satisfying summer luncheon, serve this chilled soup with crusty bread.

Start to Finish: 25 minutes **Makes:** 6 servings

1 cup dried tiny shell macaroni
   (conchigliette) or elbow macaroni
   (4 ounces)
4 cups hot-style vegetable juice, chilled
1 tablespoon lime juice or lemon juice
6 ounces cooked lump crabmeat,
   flaked, or chopped cooked chicken
   (about 1¼ cups)

2 medium nectarines, chopped
2 plum tomatoes, chopped
¼ cup chopped seeded cucumber
2 tablespoons snipped fresh basil
   Lime wedges (optional)

1

Cook pasta according to package directions. Drain. Rinse with cold water; drain again.

2

In a large bowl stir together vegetable juice and lime or lemon juice. Stir in pasta, crabmeat or chicken, nectarines, tomatoes, cucumber, and basil. Ladle soup into bowls. If desired, serve with lime wedges.

Nutrition Facts per serving: 162 calories, 1 g total fat, 28 mg cholesterol, 947 mg sodium, 28 g carbohydrate, 11 g protein.

FISH AND SHELL STEW

Give this stew a south-of-the-border slant by substituting Mexican-style stewed tomatoes for the Italian-style stewed tomatoes. (Pictured on page 141.)

Prep: 15 minutes **Cook:** 12 minutes **Makes:** 4 servings

12 ounces fresh or frozen skinless fish fillets (cod, pike, or orange roughy)

2 14-ounce cans chicken broth

1 15-ounce can chickpeas (garbanzo beans) or red kidney beans, rinsed and drained

1 cup loose-pack frozen mixed vegetables

$^3/_4$ cup dried medium shell macaroni or cavatelli (about 2 ounces)

1 medium onion, chopped

1 teaspoon dried basil or thyme, crushed

$^1/_4$ teaspoon ground black pepper

1 14$^1/_2$-ounce can Italian-style stewed tomatoes

1

Thaw fish, if frozen. Rinse fish; pat dry. Cut fish into 1-inch pieces; set aside.

2

In a large saucepan stir together broth, chickpeas or beans, frozen vegetables, pasta, onion, basil or thyme, and pepper. Bring to boiling; reduce heat. Cover and simmer for 10 minutes.

3

Stir in undrained tomatoes and fish. Return to boiling; reduce heat. Cover and simmer for 2 to 3 minutes or just until fish flakes easily with a fork.

Nutrition Facts per serving: 291 calories, 4 g total fat, 34 mg cholesterol, 1,261 mg sodium, 39 g carbohydrate, 26 g protein.

HOT AND SOUR SOUP

Adjust the level of hot and sour to be just the way you like it. Start with 1 tablespoon vinegar and a few dashes bottled hot pepper sauce. Taste the finished soup and add more of one or both ingredients to suit your taste.

Start to Finish: 25 minutes **Makes:** 2 servings

½ of a 6- or 8-ounce package refrigerated or frozen flake-style imitation crabmeat

3 cups water

1 to 2 tablespoons rice vinegar or white vinegar

Several dashes bottled hot pepper sauce

½ of a 3-ounce package Oriental-flavored ramen noodles, broken

1 small carrot, shredded

1 3-ounce can sliced mushrooms, drained

½ cup sliced water chestnuts

1 green onion, thinly sliced

1

Thaw imitation crabmeat, if frozen. Cut up any large pieces of the imitation crabmeat; set aside.

2

In a medium saucepan combine the water, vinegar, and hot pepper sauce. Bring to boiling. Stir in ramen noodles, the flavor packet from the ramen noodles, and carrot. Reduce heat. Cook, uncovered, for 3 to 5 minutes or until noodles are tender, stirring occasionally. Stir in imitation crabmeat, the mushrooms, and water chestnuts; heat through. Ladle into soup bowls. Sprinkle with green onion.

Nutrition Facts per serving: 187 calories, 5 g total fat, 13 mg cholesterol, 641 mg sodium, 26 g carbohydrate, 10 g protein.

SPRING GREEN PASTA SOUP

Asparagus and sugar snap peas contribute their bright green color and fresh flavor to the delicate soup.

Start to Finish: 30 minutes **Makes:** 4 servings

4 cups reduced-sodium chicken broth

2 cups water

2 slightly beaten eggs

2 teaspoons cooking oil

4 ounces dried angel hair pasta (capellini) or spaghettini (thin spaghetti), broken into 2-inch pieces

2 medium leeks, sliced, or $^2/_3$ cup sliced green onions

2 cloves garlic, minced

8 ounces fresh asparagus, trimmed and cut into 1-inch pieces (about 1 cup)

4 ounces fresh sugar snap peas, cut in half crosswise (about 1 cup)

2 tablespoons snipped fresh dill

2 teaspoons finely shredded lemon peel

Asparagus spears (optional)

1

In a large saucepan bring chicken broth and the water to boiling.

2

Meanwhile, in a medium skillet cook eggs in hot oil over medium heat, without stirring, for 2 to 3 minutes or until eggs are set. To remove cooked eggs, loosen edge and invert skillet over a cutting board; cut eggs into thin bite-size strips. Set aside.

3

Add pasta, leeks or green onions, and garlic to chicken broth. Boil gently, uncovered, about 3 minutes or until pasta is nearly tender. Add asparagus pieces, sugar snap peas, dill, and lemon peel. Return to boiling. Boil gently about 2 minutes more or until vegetables are crisp-tender; stir in egg strips. If desired, garnish with asparagus spears.

Nutrition Facts per serving: 235 calories, 7 g total fat, 107 mg cholesterol, 684 mg sodium, 33 g carbohydrate, 12 g protein.

CREAMY CARROT AND PASTA SOUP

Jamaican jerk seasoning adds a delightful blend of spices and herbs—and just a hint of hotness—to this creamy smooth soup.

Start to Finish: 30 minutes **Makes:** 4 servings

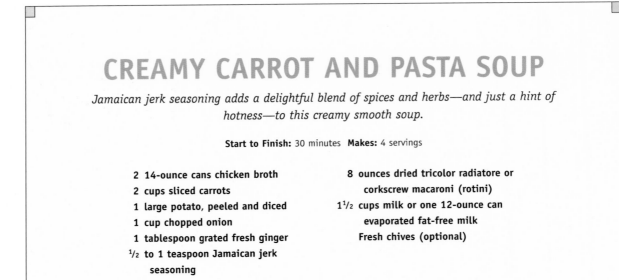

2 **14-ounce cans chicken broth**
2 **cups sliced carrots**
1 **large potato, peeled and diced**
1 **cup chopped onion**
1 **tablespoon grated fresh ginger**
$^1/_2$ **to 1 teaspoon Jamaican jerk seasoning**

8 **ounces dried tricolor radiatore or corkscrew macaroni (rotini)**
$1^1/_2$ **cups milk or one 12-ounce can evaporated fat-free milk**
Fresh chives (optional)

1

In a large saucepan combine chicken broth, carrots, potato, onion, ginger, and Jamaican jerk seasoning. Bring to boiling; reduce heat. Cover and simmer for 15 to 20 minutes or until vegetables are very tender. Cool slightly.

2

Meanwhile, cook pasta according to package directions. Drain.

3

Place one-fourth of the vegetable mixture in a food processor. Cover and process until smooth. Process remaining vegetable mixture one-fourth at a time. Return all to saucepan. Stir in cooked pasta and milk; heat through. Ladle soup into bowls. If desired, garnish with chives.

Nutrition Facts per serving: 363 calories, 4 g total fat, 8 mg cholesterol, 750 mg sodium, 65 g carbohydrate, 16 g protein.

JALAPEÑO CORN CHOWDER

Here's a great use for some leftover cooked pasta. If you don't have any leftover pasta, cook 1¹/₂ to 3 ounces small pasta according to package directions.

Start to Finish: 20 minutes **Makes:** 4 servings

3 cups frozen whole kernel corn or
    3 cups fresh corn kernels (cut from
    6 to 7 ears of corn)
1 14-ounce can chicken broth
1¹/₄ cups cooked small pasta [such as
    ditalini or tiny shell macaroni
    (conchigliette)]
1 cup milk, half-and-half, or light cream

¹/₄ of a 7-ounce jar roasted red sweet
    peppers, drained and chopped
    (¹/₄ cup)
1 or 2 fresh jalapeño peppers,*
    seeded and finely chopped
¹/₂ cup crumbled feta cheese
    (2 ounces) (optional)

1

In a blender container or food processor bowl combine half of the corn and the chicken broth. Cover and blend or process until nearly smooth.

2

In a large saucepan combine the broth mixture and the remaining corn. (If using fresh corn, bring to boiling; reduce heat. Cover and simmer for 2 to 3 minutes or until corn is crisp-tender.)

3

Stir in cooked pasta, milk, roasted peppers, and jalapeño peppers; heat through. If desired, top each serving with feta cheese.

Nutrition Facts per serving: 247 calories, 3 g total fat, 5 mg cholesterol, 363 mg sodium, 47 g carbohydrate, 11 g protein.

*Note: Because chile peppers, such as jalapeños, contain volatile oils that can burn your skin and eyes, avoid direct contact with them as much as possible. When working with chile peppers, wear plastic or rubber gloves. If your bare hands do touch the chile peppers, wash your hands and nails well with soap and warm water.

TOSS & SERVE ENTRÉES

These easy-does-it delights combine cooked pasta with a few quick-fixing ingredients.

Pasta with Ricotta and Vegetables
(see recipe, page 172)

PASTA WITH TUNA, ROASTED PEPPERS, AND ARTICHOKES

Make dinner as easy as 1-2-3! Just cook the pasta, toss with the other ingredients, and serve.

Start to Finish: 20 minutes **Makes:** 6 servings

1 pound dried tiny shell macaroni (conchigliette) or tiny bow ties (tripolini)

1 7-ounce jar roasted red sweet peppers, drained and cut into thin strips

1 6½-ounce can tuna, drained

1 6-ounce jar marinated artichoke hearts, drained and halved

2 tablespoons olive oil

1 tablespoon capers

1 tablespoon snipped fresh parsley

1 teaspoon bottled minced garlic

2 teaspoons balsamic vinegar

½ teaspoon salt

¼ teaspoon freshly ground black pepper

1
Cook pasta according to package directions. Drain.

2
Meanwhile, in a large serving bowl combine roasted red peppers, tuna, artichoke hearts, olive oil, capers, parsley, and garlic. Add the hot cooked pasta. Toss to coat all ingredients.

3
Add balsamic vinegar, salt, and black pepper; toss again.

Nutrition Facts per serving: 415 calories, 10 g total fat, 5 mg cholesterol, 476 mg sodium, 61 g carbohydrate, 19 g protein.

HERBED TURKEY AND BROCCOLI

This is one-pan cooking at its best. Use a Dutch oven or large saucepan to cook the pasta so there is plenty of room to toss all the ingredients together.

Start to Finish: 20 minutes **Makes:** 4 servings

8 ounces dried linguine or spaghetti, broken in half

3 cups small broccoli florets

1 8-ounce container soft-style cream cheese with garlic and herbs

$2/3$ cup milk

$1/4$ teaspoon coarsely ground black pepper

6 ounces sliced smoked turkey breast, cut into bite-size strips

Milk (optional)

1

In a Dutch oven or large saucepan cook pasta according to package directions, adding broccoli for the last 3 minutes of cooking. Drain and set aside.

2

In the same hot Dutch oven or saucepan combine cream cheese, the $2/3$ cup milk, and the pepper. Cook and stir over low heat just until cream cheese is melted. Add pasta-broccoli mixture and turkey. Toss to coat all ingredients. If necessary, stir in enough additional milk to make desired consistency.

Nutrition Facts per serving: 516 calories, 21 g total fat, 81 mg cholesterol, 675 mg sodium, 57 g carbohydrate, 25 g protein.

FRESH PASTA WITH SUN-DRIED TOMATO PESTO

The flavors of pine nuts and dried tomatoes marry perfectly in this simple pesto.

Start to Finish: 20 minutes **Makes:** 6 servings

2 9-ounce packages refrigerated linguine or fettuccine
$\frac{1}{2}$ cup dried tomatoes (not oil-packed) or $\frac{1}{3}$ cup dried tomato bits
$\frac{1}{2}$ cup hot water
$\frac{1}{2}$ cup pine nuts
$\frac{1}{3}$ cup olive oil

$\frac{1}{4}$ teaspoon salt
$\frac{1}{4}$ teaspoon dried thyme, crushed
$\frac{1}{2}$ teaspoon freshly ground black pepper
$\frac{1}{4}$ cup freshly grated Parmesan cheese
1 tablespoon minced garlic

1

Cook pasta according to package directions. Drain, reserving $\frac{1}{2}$ cup cooking liquid. Return pasta and $\frac{1}{2}$ cup cooking liquid to saucepan. Cover; keep warm.

2

Meanwhile, in a small bowl combine the dried tomatoes and the hot water. Let stand for 10 minutes. Drain tomatoes, squeezing out as much liquid as possible. Place tomatoes in a blender container. Add pine nuts, oil, salt, thyme, and pepper. Cover and blend until smooth.

3

Stir the Parmesan cheese and garlic into tomato mixture in blender container. Toss tomato mixture with pasta and the reserved cooking liquid.

Nutrition Facts per serving: 523 calories, 27 g total fat, 106 mg cholesterol, 589 mg sodium, 51 g carbohydrate, 22 g protein.

WILTED GREENS WITH DRIED TOMATOES AND PASTA

Here's a quick solution to the what-to-fix-for-dinner dilemma—pasta tossed with spinach, dried tomatoes, and feta cheese.

Start to Finish: 25 minutes **Makes:** 4 servings

- 6 ounces dried orecchiette or medium shell macaroni
- 4 cloves garlic, thinly sliced
- $1/3$ cup oil-packed dried tomatoes
- 6 cups torn fresh spinach
- $1/8$ teaspoon salt
- $1/8$ teaspoon coarsely ground black pepper
- $1/4$ cup crumbled feta cheese (1 ounce)

1

Cook pasta according to package directions, adding garlic for the last 4 minutes of cooking. Drain; return pasta and garlic to saucepan.

2

Meanwhile, drain tomatoes, reserving 1 tablespoon of the oil. Cut tomatoes into strips. Add tomato strips, reserved oil, spinach, salt, and pepper to pasta in saucepan; toss gently to combine. Cover saucepan for 2 minutes or until spinach is slightly wilted. To serve, sprinkle with feta cheese.

Nutrition Facts per serving: 248 calories, 6 g total fat, 14 mg cholesterol, 336 mg sodium, 40 g carbohydrate, 11 g protein.

PASTA WITH RICOTTA AND VEGETABLES

Fresh basil and thyme complement the fresh vegetables in this meatless main dish.
(Pictured on page 165.)

Start to Finish: 20 minutes **Makes:** 4 servings

8 ounces dried penne (mostaccioli) or cut ziti
2$^{1}/_{2}$ cups broccoli florets
1$^{1}/_{2}$ cups fresh asparagus or green beans cut into 1-inch pieces
2 large red and/or yellow tomatoes
1 cup light ricotta cheese
$^{1}/_{4}$ cup snipped fresh basil
4 teaspoons snipped fresh thyme

4 teaspoons balsamic vinegar
1 tablespoon olive oil
1 clove garlic, minced
$^{1}/_{2}$ teaspoon salt
$^{1}/_{2}$ teaspoon freshly ground black pepper
2 tablespoons grated Parmesan or Romano cheese
Fresh thyme sprigs (optional)

1

Cook pasta according to package directions, adding broccoli and asparagus or beans for the last 3 minutes of cooking. Drain.

2

Meanwhile, place a fine strainer over a large bowl. Cut tomatoes in half; squeeze seeds and juice into strainer. With the back of a spoon, push seeds to extract juice; discard seeds. Add ricotta cheese, basil, snipped thyme, vinegar, oil, garlic, salt, and pepper to tomato juice; mix well. Chop tomatoes; stir into ricotta mixture.

3

In a large serving bowl combine hot pasta-vegetable mixture and ricotta mixture. Toss to coat all ingredients. Sprinkle with Parmesan or Romano cheese. If desired, garnish with thyme sprigs.

Nutrition Facts per serving: 368 calories, 8 g total fat, 12 mg cholesterol, 393 mg sodium, 57 g carbohydrate, 19 g protein.

PASTA WITH CHÈVRE

Rich, meaty Greek black olives, such as kalamatas, add a touch of the Mediterranean to this simple combo. However, any ripe olives will work.

Start to Finish: 25 minutes **Makes:** 4 servings

- 8 ounces dried cavatelli or medium shell macaroni
- 2 medium tomatoes, chopped
- 1 yellow sweet pepper, cut into bite-size pieces
- 4 ounces crumbled semisoft mild goat cheese (chèvre) or crumbled feta cheese
- 1/3 cup pitted, chopped Greek black olives or ripe olives
- 2 tablespoons snipped fresh basil
- 2 tablespoons olive oil
- 1/4 teaspoon coarsely ground black pepper (optional)

1

Cook pasta according to package directions. Drain. Return pasta to saucepan.

2

Add tomatoes, sweet pepper, cheese, olives, basil, and olive oil to saucepan. Toss gently to combine. Transfer to a warm serving dish. If desired, sprinkle with black pepper.

Nutrition Facts per serving: 402 calories, 18 g total fat, 25 mg cholesterol, 216 mg sodium, 49 g carbohydrate, 14 g protein.

PASTA WITH PESTO-TOMATO SAUCE

Visit a farmer's market—or your garden—to get ripe tomatoes that are nice and juicy.

Start to Finish: 25 minutes **Makes:** 4 servings

$2^2/_3$ cups dried penne (mostaccioli) or
    cut ziti (8 ounces)
$1/_4$ cup pine nuts or chopped almonds
$1/_4$ cup grated Romano or Parmesan
    cheese
2 cloves garlic, minced
2 cups loosely packed fresh basil
    leaves, chopped

$1/_4$ cup olive oil
$1^1/_2$ pounds tomatoes, peeled, seeded,
    and chopped
$1/_2$ teaspoon salt
$1/_8$ teaspoon ground black pepper
Fresh basil sprigs (optional)
Pine nuts (optional)

1
Cook pasta according to package directions. Drain. Cover and keep warm.

2
Meanwhile, for sauce, in a food processor bowl combine the $1/_4$ cup pine nuts or almonds, Romano or Parmesan cheese, and garlic. Cover and process until chopped. Add about half of the basil leaves and the oil; cover and process until basil is chopped, stopping the machine occasionally to scrape the side. Add remaining basil leaves; cover and process until basil is chopped, stopping the machine occasionally to scrape side. Stir in tomatoes, salt, and pepper.

3
On a serving platter top hot cooked pasta with sauce. If desired, garnish with basil sprigs and additional pine nuts.

Nutrition Facts per serving: 459 calories, 22 g total fat, 5 mg cholesterol, 400 mg sodium, 55 g carbohydrate, 14 g protein.

BOW TIES WITH ASPARAGUS

As the seasons change, use whatever vegetables are available at your market. Zucchini, tomatoes, green beans, carrots, and yellow summer squash all work well.

Start to Finish: 25 minutes **Makes:** 4 servings

1 pound dried large bow ties (farfalle) or wagon wheel macaroni (ruote)

1 pound thin fresh asparagus, trimmed and cut into 2-inch pieces

¼ cup olive oil

1 teaspoon grated lemon peel

¼ cup lemon juice

¼ teaspoon bottled minced garlic

1 teaspoon Dijon-style mustard

½ teaspoon salt

½ teaspoon freshly ground black pepper

1 cup sliced radishes

1 cup loose-pack frozen baby peas, thawed

1 green onion, thinly sliced

2 tablespoons snipped fresh parsley

1

Cook pasta according to package directions, adding asparagus for the last 3 minutes of cooking. Drain. Rinse pasta and asparagus with cold water; drain again.

2

For dressing, in a large bowl whisk together olive oil, lemon peel, lemon juice, minced garlic, mustard, salt, and pepper. Add pasta-asparagus mixture, radishes, peas, green onion, and parsley. Toss to coat all ingredients.

Nutrition Facts per serving: 605 calories, 16 g total fat, 0 mg cholesterol, 393 mg sodium, 97 g carbohydrate, 20 g protein.

CREAMY THREE-CHEESE AND TOASTED WALNUT PASTA

The heat from the pasta and a little of the cooking liquid melts the ricotta, Gorgonzola, and Parmesan into a rich, creamy sauce.

Start to Finish: 15 minutes **Makes:** 6 servings

1 pound dried tricolor or plain large
   bow ties (farfalle) or penne
   (mostaccioli)
²/₃ cup ricotta cheese
¹/₂ cup crumbled Gorgonzola or other
   blue cheese (2 ounces)
¹/₄ cup freshly grated Parmesan cheese
   (1 ounce)

2 tablespoons butter or margarine,
   softened
³/₄ cup loose-pack frozen peas, thawed
³/₄ cup walnuts, toasted and chopped
¹/₂ teaspoon salt
¹/₂ teaspoon freshly ground black
   pepper

1
Cook pasta according to package directions. Drain, reserving ¹/₄ cup of the hot cooking liquid.

2
Meanwhile, in a large serving bowl stir together ricotta cheese, Gorgonzola cheese, Parmesan cheese, and butter or margarine. Stir in peas, walnuts, salt, and pepper.

3
Quickly stir in the reserved cooking liquid. Add the hot pasta. Toss to coat all ingredients.

Nutrition Facts per serving: 540 calories, 23 g total fat, 38 mg cholesterol, 531 mg sodium, 63 g carbohydrate, 20 g protein.

PENNE SALAD WITH ITALIAN BEANS AND GORGONZOLA

Italian green beans are wider and flatter than regular green beans. Use the fresh beans when they are in season. Other times, use frozen beans.

Start to Finish: 25 minutes **Makes:** 4 servings

2 cups dried penne (mostaccioli), cut ziti, or wagon wheel macaroni (ruote) (6 ounces)

8 ounces fresh Italian green beans,* bias-sliced into 1-inch pieces

1/3 cup bottled fat-free Italian salad dressing

1 tablespoon snipped fresh tarragon or 1/2 teaspoon dried tarragon, crushed

1/2 teaspoon freshly ground black pepper

2 cups torn radicchio or 1 cup finely shredded red cabbage

4 cups fresh sorrel or spinach leaves

1/2 cup crumbled Gorgonzola or other blue cheese (2 ounces)

1

Cook pasta according to package directions, adding green beans for the last 7 minutes of cooking. Drain. Rinse pasta and beans with cold water; drain again.

2

In a large bowl combine Italian salad dressing, tarragon, and pepper. Add pasta mixture and radicchio. Toss gently to coat all ingredients.

3

To serve, divide sorrel or spinach leaves among 4 shallow bowls or 4 dinner plates. Top with pasta mixture. Sprinkle with Gorgonzola cheese.

Nutrition Facts per serving: 269 calories, 6 g total fat, 13 mg cholesterol, 566 mg sodium, 42 g carbohydrate, 12 g protein.

*Note: One 9-ounce package frozen Italian green beans, thawed, may be substituted for the fresh beans. Add frozen and thawed beans to the boiling pasta for the last 4 minutes of cooking.

MAIN-DISH SALADS

Ideal for lunch, a light supper, or to take to a picnic or potluck, these hearty pasta salads are the best ever.

Chicken-and-Melon Stuffed Shells
(see recipe, page 187)

TERIYAKI CHICKEN NOODLE SALAD

Ramen noodles add a delightful crunch, and oranges add a hint of sweetness.

Start to Finish: 30 minutes **Makes:** 4 servings

1 3-ounce package chicken- or Oriental-flavored ramen noodles
¼ cup rice vinegar or white wine vinegar
2 tablespoons orange juice
2 tablespoons salad oil
Few dashes bottled hot pepper sauce
6 cups torn mixed salad greens

2 cups fresh vegetables (such as bean sprouts, halved pea pods, or sliced carrots, yellow summer squash, zucchini, cucumber, and/or onions)
2 oranges, peeled, halved, and thinly sliced
2 tablespoons cooking oil
12 ounces skinless, boneless chicken breasts, cut into thin bite-size strips
Coarsely ground black pepper

1

For dressing, in a screw-top jar combine the flavor packet from the ramen noodles, the vinegar, orange juice, salad oil, and hot pepper sauce. Cover and shake well; set aside.

2

In a large salad bowl combine salad greens, desired vegetables, and orange slices; toss gently to mix. Break ramen noodles into pieces; add to salad. Cover and refrigerate until serving time (up to 1 hour).

3

Heat oil in a wok or large skillet. Add chicken; stir-fry for 2 to 3 minutes or until no longer pink.

4

While chicken is cooking, pour the dressing over the salad mixture; toss gently to coat. Let stand about 5 minutes to soften noodles, tossing occasionally.

5

Add chicken and pan juices to salad; toss gently. Sprinkle with pepper. Serve immediately.

Nutrition Facts per serving: 351 calories, 17 g total fat, 45 mg cholesterol, 521 mg sodium, 30 g carbohydrate, 21 g protein.

FRUITED CHICKEN-PASTA SALAD

Dress the salad with your choice of regular or a flavored buttermilk ranch dressing.

Start to Finish: 25 minutes **Makes:** 4 or 5 servings

1 cup dried medium shell macaroni or
  elbow macaroni (3 ounces)

1½ cups chopped cooked chicken or
  turkey (about 8 ounces)

1 11-ounce can mandarin orange
  sections, drained

1 cup seedless red or green grapes,
  halved

1 8-ounce can sliced water chestnuts,
  drained

½ cup sliced celery

½ cup bottled buttermilk ranch salad
  dressing

⅛ teaspoon ground black pepper

  Milk

  Leaf lettuce

1

Cook pasta according to package directions. Drain. Rinse with cold water; drain again.

2

In a large bowl combine pasta, chicken or turkey, mandarin orange sections, grapes, water chestnuts, and celery.

3

For dressing, in a small bowl combine buttermilk ranch salad dressing and pepper. Pour dressing over chicken mixture. Toss gently to coat. (If desired, cover and chill in the refrigerator for up to 24 hours. Before serving, if necessary, stir in enough milk to moisten.) Serve salad on lettuce-lined dinner plates.

Nutrition Facts per serving: 387 calories, 22 g total fat, 37 mg cholesterol, 302 mg sodium, 31 g carbohydrate, 16 g protein.

CHICKEN-AND-MELON-STUFFED SHELLS

Next time you grill, cook an extra chicken breast so a couple of nights later you can make this refreshing salad. (Pictured on page 183.)

Start to Finish: 25 minutes **Makes:** 4 servings

8 dried jumbo shell macaroni
   (conchiglioni)
1 medium cantaloupe, halved and
   seeded
6 to 8 ounces skinless, boneless
   chicken breast, grilled

½ cup finely diced honeydew melon
¼ cup plain low-fat yogurt
1 tablespoon snipped fresh chives
2 tablespoons lemon juice
1 teaspoon Dijon-style mustard
   Fresh thyme sprigs (optional)

1
Cook pasta shells according to package directions. Drain; rinse with cold water. Drain again.

2
Meanwhile, cut each cantaloupe half into thirds; cover 4 slices and refrigerate. Peel and dice remaining 2 slices. Cut grilled chicken breast into small pieces.

3
In a large bowl combine diced cantaloupe, chicken, honeydew, yogurt, chives, lemon juice, and mustard. Spoon about ¼ cup of the mixture into each pasta shell. Arrange 2 filled shells and a chilled cantaloupe slice in each of 4 bowls or plates. If desired, garnish with thyme sprigs.

Nutrition Facts per serving: 176 calories, 2 g total fat, 26 mg cholesterol, 55 mg sodium, 28 g carbohydrate, 14 g protein.

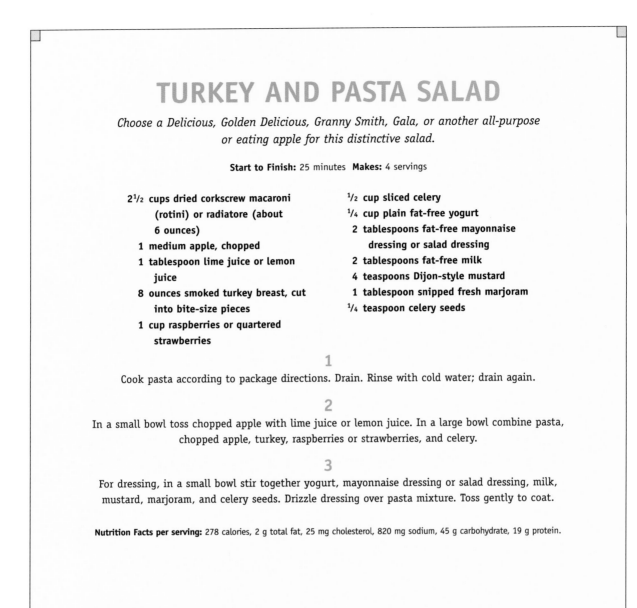

TURKEY AND PASTA SALAD

Choose a Delicious, Golden Delicious, Granny Smith, Gala, or another all-purpose or eating apple for this distinctive salad.

Start to Finish: 25 minutes **Makes:** 4 servings

2$\frac{1}{2}$ cups dried corkscrew macaroni (rotini) or radiatore (about 6 ounces)
1 medium apple, chopped
1 tablespoon lime juice or lemon juice
8 ounces smoked turkey breast, cut into bite-size pieces
1 cup raspberries or quartered strawberries

$\frac{1}{2}$ cup sliced celery
$\frac{1}{4}$ cup plain fat-free yogurt
2 tablespoons fat-free mayonnaise dressing or salad dressing
2 tablespoons fat-free milk
4 teaspoons Dijon-style mustard
1 tablespoon snipped fresh marjoram
$\frac{1}{4}$ teaspoon celery seeds

1

Cook pasta according to package directions. Drain. Rinse with cold water; drain again.

2

In a small bowl toss chopped apple with lime juice or lemon juice. In a large bowl combine pasta, chopped apple, turkey, raspberries or strawberries, and celery.

3

For dressing, in a small bowl stir together yogurt, mayonnaise dressing or salad dressing, milk, mustard, marjoram, and celery seeds. Drizzle dressing over pasta mixture. Toss gently to coat.

Nutrition Facts per serving: 278 calories, 2 g total fat, 25 mg cholesterol, 820 mg sodium, 45 g carbohydrate, 19 g protein.

HAM AND CHUTNEY PASTA SALAD

To quick-chill the macaroni, drain it in a colander that's set in the kitchen sink. Then, run cold water over the pasta in the colander for a minute or two. Drain well before using.

Start to Finish: 25 minutes **Makes:** 4 servings

2½ cups dried medium shell macaroni
    or 2 cups dried elbow macaroni
    (8 ounces)
½ cup chutney
½ cup mayonnaise or salad dressing
2 green onions, sliced

⅛ teaspoon coarsely ground black
    pepper
1½ cups cubed cooked ham (8 ounces)
4 lettuce leaves
    Cherry tomato wedges (optional)

1

Cook pasta according to package directions; drain. Rinse with cold water. Drain again.

2

Meanwhile, cut up any large pieces of chutney. In a small bowl stir together the chutney, mayonnaise or salad dressing, green onions, and pepper.

3

In a large bowl toss together the pasta, chutney mixture, and ham. Line 4 dinner plates with lettuce leaves. Serve ham mixture on lettuce-lined plates. If desired, garnish with cherry tomato wedges.

Nutrition Facts per serving: 580 calories, 26 g total fat, 46 mg cholesterol, 850 mg sodium, 66 g carbohydrate, 20 g protein.

SALMON-PASTA SALAD

A day or two before you want to make this flavorful salad, put the can of salmon in the refrigerator to chill.

Start to Finish: 30 minutes **Makes:** 4 servings

1 cup dried corkscrew macaroni
  (rotini) or medium shell macaroni
  (about 3 ounces)
1½ cups broccoli florets
4 ounces Gruyère or Swiss cheese, cut
  into thin bite-size strips
¼ cup sliced radishes
⅔ cup mayonnaise or salad dressing
1 tablespoon snipped fresh basil or
  1 teaspoon dried basil, crushed

2 teaspoons white wine
  Worcestershire sauce
⅛ teaspoon garlic salt
1 to 2 tablespoons milk
1 14¾-ounce can salmon, chilled
  Leaf lettuce
  Pineapple sage flowers or other
  fresh herb sprigs (optional)

1

Cook pasta according to package directions, adding broccoli for the last 4 minutes of cooking. Drain pasta and broccoli. Rinse with cold water; drain again.

2

In a large bowl combine pasta-broccoli mixture, cheese, and radishes.

3

For dressing, in a small bowl stir together mayonnaise or salad dressing, basil, white wine Worcestershire sauce, garlic salt, and enough of the milk to make desired consistency. Pour dressing over pasta mixture. Toss lightly to mix. (If desired, cover and chill in the refrigerator for up to 24 hours. Before serving, if necessary, stir in enough additional milk to moisten.)

4

Drain and flake salmon, discarding skin and bones. Fold salmon into salad mixture.

5

Line 4 dinner plates with lettuce. Divide salad among lettuce-lined plates. If desired, garnish with pineapple sage flowers or other herb sprigs.

Nutrition Facts per serving: 641 calories, 47 g total fat, 101 mg cholesterol, 999 mg sodium, 19 g carbohydrate, 36 g protein.

MEXICAN FIESTA SALAD

When corn on the cob is in season, use ¹/₂ cup fresh corn kernels in this spunky salad, and save a few of the corn husks to line the plates.

Start to Finish: 30 minutes **Makes:** 4 servings

2 cups dried penne (mostaccioli) or corkscrew macaroni (rotini) (about 6 ounces)
¹/₂ cup frozen whole kernel corn
¹/₂ cup light dairy sour cream
¹/₃ cup mild or medium bottled chunky salsa
1 tablespoon snipped fresh cilantro

1 tablespoon lime juice
1 15-ounce can black beans, rinsed and drained
3 medium plum tomatoes, chopped
1 medium zucchini, chopped
¹/₂ cup shredded sharp cheddar cheese (2 ounces)

1

Cook pasta according to package directions, adding the corn for the last 5 minutes of cooking. Drain pasta and corn. Rinse with cold water; drain again.

2

Meanwhile, for dressing, in a small bowl stir together sour cream, salsa, cilantro, and lime juice. Set dressing aside.

3

In a large bowl combine pasta-corn mixture, black beans, tomatoes, zucchini, and cheese. Pour dressing over pasta mixture. Toss lightly to coat. (If desired, cover and chill in the refrigerator for up to 24 hours. Before serving, if necessary, stir in enough milk to moisten.)

Nutrition Facts per serving: 373 calories, 9 g total fat, 19 mg cholesterol, 470 mg sodium, 61 g carbohydrate, 20 g protein.

TORTELLINI-VEGETABLE SALAD

To keep prep time to a minimum, purchase packaged torn mixed salad greens.

Start to Finish: 20 minutes **Makes:** 4 servings

1 9-ounce package refrigerated
   cheese-filled tortellini or ravioli
6 cups torn mixed salad greens
1½ cups sliced fresh mushrooms
1 medium red or yellow sweet pepper,
   cut into bite-size strips
¼ cup snipped fresh basil
¼ cup white wine vinegar or white
   vinegar

2 tablespoons water
2 tablespoons olive oil
2 teaspoons sugar
2 cloves garlic, minced
¼ teaspoon ground black pepper
½ cup purchased fat-free toasted
   garlic-and-onion croutons

1

Cook pasta according to package directions, except omit any oil or salt. Drain. Rinse with cold water;
drain again.

2

In a large bowl combine pasta, mixed salad greens, mushrooms, sweet pepper, and basil.

3

For dressing, in a screw-top jar combine vinegar, the water, oil, sugar, garlic, and black pepper. Cover
and shake well. Pour over pasta mixture. Toss to coat.

4

To serve, divide the pasta mixture among 4 bowls or plates. Pass croutons.

Nutrition Facts per serving: 302 calories, 12 g total fat, 30 mg cholesterol, 288 mg sodium, 40 g carbohydrate, 12 g protein.

SOUTH-OF-THE-BORDER BEAN AND PASTA SALAD

Kick up the flavor a notch by using Monterey Jack cheese with jalapeño peppers.

Start to Finish: 30 minutes **Makes:** 4 servings

1 cup dried wagon wheel macaroni
(ruote) or elbow macaroni
(3 to 4 ounces)
1 15-ounce can pinto beans, rinsed
and drained
1 cup jicama cut into thin bite-size
strips
1 cup cubed cheddar or Monterey Jack
cheese (4 ounces)
1 cup chopped seeded tomato

1 4-ounce can diced green chile
peppers, drained
2 tablespoons finely chopped onion
1 recipe Salsa Dressing
4 cups shredded leaf lettuce
1 medium avocado, seeded, peeled,
and sliced
Blue corn tortilla chips or tortilla
chips (optional)

1

Cook pasta according to package directions. Drain pasta. Rinse with cold water; drain again.

2

In a large bowl combine pasta, pinto beans, jicama, cheese, tomato, chile peppers, and onion. Toss lightly to mix. Pour Salsa Dressing over pasta mixture. Toss lightly to coat. (If desired, cover and chill in the refrigerator for up to 24 hours. Before serving, if necessary, stir in enough milk to moisten.)

3

To serve, divide shredded lettuce among 4 dinner plates. Spoon pasta mixture onto shredded lettuce. Top with sliced avocado. If desired, garnish with tortilla chips.

Salsa Dressing: In a small bowl stir together ⅓ cup plain yogurt, ⅓ cup mayonnaise or salad dressing, and 3 tablespoons bottled salsa.

Nutrition Facts per serving: 552 calories, 34 g total fat, 42 mg cholesterol, 823 mg sodium, 47 g carbohydrate, 21 g protein.

GRILLED VEGETABLE SALAD WITH GARLIC DRESSING

Get a head start on this meatless main-dish salad by grilling the vegetables and cooking the pasta up to 24 hours ahead. Cover and refrigerate the vegetables and pasta until needed.

Start to Finish: 30 minutes **Makes:** 4 servings

4 or 5 yellow sunburst or pattypan squash
2 red and/or yellow sweet peppers
2 Japanese eggplants, halved lengthwise
1 medium zucchini or yellow summer squash, halved lengthwise
1 tablespoon olive oil

2 cups dried tortiglioni or rigatoni (about 5 ounces)
1 recipe Roasted Garlic Dressing
¾ cup cubed fontina cheese (3 ounces)
1 to 2 tablespoons snipped fresh flat-leaf parsley
Fresh flat-leaf parsley sprigs

1

In a covered medium saucepan cook sunburst or pattypan squash in a small amount of boiling water for 3 minutes; drain. Halve sweet peppers lengthwise; remove and discard stems, seeds, and membranes. Brush sunburst or pattypan squash, sweet peppers, eggplants, and zucchini or yellow summer squash with oil. Grill vegetables on grill rack of an uncovered grill directly over medium-hot coals for 8 to 12 minutes or until vegetables are tender, turning occasionally. Remove vegetables from grill; cool slightly. Cut vegetables into 1-inch pieces.

2

Meanwhile, cook pasta according to package directions. Drain. Rinse with cold water; drain again.

3

In a large bowl combine pasta and grilled vegetables. Pour Roasted Garlic Dressing over salad. Toss lightly to coat. Stir in cheese; sprinkle with snipped parsley. If desired, garnish with parsley sprigs.

Roasted Garlic Dressing: In a screw-top jar combine 3 tablespoons balsamic vinegar or red wine vinegar, 2 tablespoons olive oil, 1 tablespoon water, 1 teaspoon bottled roasted minced garlic, ¼ teaspoon salt, and ¼ teaspoon ground black pepper. Cover and shake well.

Nutrition Facts per serving: 369 calories, 19 g total fat, 61 mg cholesterol, 317 mg sodium, 40 g carbohydrate, 12 g protein.

FONTINA AND MELON SALAD

Take advantage of a sunny day by serving lunch on the patio. Start with this delectable salad, pass an assortment of crisp breadsticks, and top off the meal with your favorite ice cream.

Start to Finish: 25 minutes **Makes:** 4 servings

3 cups dried large bow ties (farfalle) or 2 cups dried medium shell macaroni (6 ounces)

2 cups cantaloupe and/or honeydew melon chunks

1 cup cubed fontina or Swiss cheese (4 ounces)

$\frac{1}{3}$ cup bottled fat-free poppy seed salad dressing

1 to 2 tablespoons snipped fresh mint

2 cups watercress, stems removed

4 cantaloupe and/or honeydew melon halves (optional)

1

Cook pasta according to package directions. Drain. Rinse with cold water; drain again.

2

In a large bowl toss together pasta, cantaloupe and/or honeydew chunks, and cheese. In a small bowl combine salad dressing and mint; pour over pasta mixture. Toss gently to coat. (If desired, cover and chill in the refrigerator for up to 24 hours.)

3

Stir watercress into pasta mixture. If desired, serve salad in cantaloupe and/or honeydew melon halves.

Nutrition Facts per serving: 319 calories, 11 g total fat, 73 mg cholesterol, 309 mg sodium, 41 g carbohydrate, 14 g protein.

TORTELLINI-CAESAR SALAD

The addition of cheese-filled tortellini transforms Caesar salad into a mouthwatering main dish.

Start to Finish: 40 minutes **Makes:** 4 servings

1 egg
1/3 cup chicken broth
3 anchovy fillets, mashed
3 tablespoons olive oil or salad oil
2 tablespoons lemon juice
Few dashes white wine
Worcestershire sauce
12 ounces fresh asparagus spears,
trimmed and cut into 1-inch
pieces, or one 10-ounce package
frozen cut asparagus

2 cups frozen or refrigerated
cheese-filled tortellini or ravioli
(about 7 ounces)
1 clove garlic, halved
10 cups torn romaine
1/2 cup Italian Croutons or purchased
croutons
1/4 cup finely shredded Parmesan
cheese (1 ounce)
Coarsely ground black pepper

1

For dressing, in a blender container or food processor bowl combine egg, chicken broth, anchovy fillets, oil, lemon juice, and Worcestershire sauce. Cover and blend or process until smooth. Transfer dressing to a small saucepan. Cook and stir dressing over low heat for 8 to 10 minutes or until thickened. Do not boil. Transfer to a small bowl. Cover surface with plastic wrap. Place in freezer to chill for 20 minutes, stirring often (do not freeze). (Or chill in the refrigerator for up to 24 hours.)

2

Meanwhile, in a covered medium saucepan cook fresh asparagus in a small amount of boiling water for 4 to 8 minutes or until tender. (Or cook frozen asparagus according to package directions.) Cook pasta according to package directions. Drain. Rinse with cold water; drain again. Set aside.

3

To serve, rub the inside of a wooden salad bowl with the cut sides of the garlic clove. Discard garlic. Add asparagus, pasta, romaine, Italian Croutons, and Parmesan cheese to salad bowl. Pour dressing over salad. Toss lightly to coat. Spoon onto 4 dinner plates. Sprinkle pepper over each serving.

Italian Croutons: Cut four 1/2-inch slices French bread into 3/4-inch cubes; set aside. In a large skillet melt 1/4 cup margarine or butter. Remove from heat. Stir in 3 tablespoons grated Parmesan cheese; 1/2 teaspoon dried Italian seasoning, crushed; and 1/8 teaspoon garlic powder. Add bread cubes, stirring until cubes are coated. Spread bread cubes in a single layer in a shallow baking pan. Bake in a 300°F oven for 10 minutes; stir. Bake for 5 to 10 minutes more or until bread cubes are dry and crisp. Cool completely before using. To store, place in an airtight container and store in the refrigerator for up to 1 month. Bring to room temperature before serving. Makes about 2 cups.

Nutrition Facts per serving: 434 calories, 21 g total fat, 97 mg cholesterol, 711 mg sodium, 42 g carbohydrate, 21 g protein.

PASTA-FRUIT SALAD

If you have a little extra time, quick chill the pasta-fruit mixture in the freezer for up to 30 minutes. Add the dressing just before serving.

Start to Finish: 30 minutes **Makes:** 4 servings

- 4 ounces dried pasta ruffles, medium shell macaroni, or corkscrew macaroni (rotini)
- 1 16-ounce can apricot halves in light syrup or one 16-ounce can peach slices in light syrup, drained
- 1 8-ounce can pineapple tidbits (juice pack) or one 11-ounce can mandarin orange sections, drained
- 1 cup seedless red or green grapes, halved

- $3/4$ cup shredded cheddar cheese (3 ounces)
- $1/4$ cup broken pecans or walnuts
- $1/2$ of an 8-ounce carton vanilla yogurt
- 1 tablespoon frozen orange juice concentrate
- $1/8$ teaspoon ground nutmeg
  Lettuce leaves

1

Cook pasta according to package directions; drain. Rinse with cold water. Drain again.

2

Meanwhile, cut up apricot halves or peach slices. In a large bowl toss together apricots or peaches, pineapple tidbits or orange sections, grapes, cheese, and pecans or walnuts. Add pasta. Toss to mix.

3

For dressing, in a small bowl stir together yogurt, orange juice concentrate, and nutmeg. Add dressing to pasta mixture; toss to coat. Line 4 dinner plates with lettuce leaves. Divide salad among lettuce-lined plates.

Nutrition Facts per serving: 411 calories, 13 g total fat, 24 mg cholesterol, 163 mg sodium, 65 g carbohydrate, 12 g protein.

DELI-STYLE PASTA SALAD

Combine cheese-filled tortellini, a medley of fresh vegetables, and a shake-together herb vinaigrette and you've got a super salad.

Start to Finish: 25 minutes **Makes:** 4 servings

1/2 of a 16-ounce package (about 2 cups) frozen cheese-filled tortellini or one 9-ounce package refrigerated cheese-filled tortellini
1 1/2 cups broccoli florets
1 large carrot, bias sliced
1/4 cup white wine vinegar
2 tablespoons olive oil
1 teaspoon dried Italian seasoning, crushed

1 teaspoon Dijon-style mustard
1/4 teaspoon ground black pepper
1/8 teaspoon garlic powder
1 medium red or yellow sweet pepper, cut into thin strips
Fresh chives with blossoms (optional)

1

In a large saucepan cook pasta according to package directions, except omit any oil or salt and add broccoli and carrot for the last 3 minutes of cooking. Drain. Rinse with cold water; drain again.

2

Meanwhile, for dressing, in a screw-top jar combine the vinegar, oil, Italian seasoning, mustard, black pepper, and garlic powder. Cover and shake well. Set aside.

3

In a large bowl combine the pasta mixture and sweet pepper. Shake dressing. Pour the dressing over pasta mixture; toss gently to coat. If desired, garnish with chives with blossoms.

Nutrition Facts per serving: 305 calories, 12 g total fat, 30 mg cholesterol, 315 mg sodium, 41 g carbohydrate, 13 g protein.

THREE-CHEESE ORZO SALAD

Orzo, a rice-shaped pasta, is also known as rosamarina.

Start to Finish: 30 minutes **Makes:** 8 servings

2 cups sugar snap peas, ends trimmed
1¼ cups dried orzo (rosamarina)
1 6-ounce jar marinated artichoke
   hearts
2 cups red or yellow cherry tomatoes
   and/or baby pear tomatoes, halved
1 cup cubed mozzarella cheese
   (4 ounces)
1 4-ounce package crumbled feta or
   peppercorn feta cheese (1 cup)

¼ cup shredded Parmesan cheese
   (1 ounce)
¼ cup white wine vinegar
¼ cup water
2 teaspoons sugar
1 tablespoon snipped fresh dill or
   1 teaspoon dried dill

1

In a large saucepan cook sugar snap peas in a large amount of boiling, lightly salted water for
1 minute. Using a slotted spoon, transfer peas to a colander. Rinse under cold water; drain. Set aside.

2

Add orzo to the boiling water in same saucepan. Boil for 8 to 10 minutes or until tender but still firm;
drain. Rinse with cold water; drain again.

3

Meanwhile, drain artichoke hearts, reserving marinade. Cut artichokes into bite-size pieces. In a large
bowl toss together artichoke hearts, sugar snap peas, orzo, tomatoes, and cheeses.

4

For dressing, in a screw-top jar combine reserved artichoke marinade, the vinegar, the water, sugar, and
dill. Cover and shake well. Pour dressing over salad. Toss lightly to coat. (If desired, cover and chill in
the refrigerator for up to 24 hours.)

Nutrition Facts per serving: 233 calories, 8 g total fat, 23 mg cholesterol, 336 mg sodium, 28 g carbohydrate, 12 g protein.

SIDE DISHES

Accent all of your favorite main dishes with one of these side-dish pasta and vegetable combos.

Garlic Asparagus and Pasta with Lemon Cream
(see recipe, page 220)

FLORENTINE PASTA SALAD

This colorful side dish gets most of its full flavor from refrigerated pesto sauce.

Start to Finish: 25 minutes **Makes:** 4 servings

2 ounces dried linguine or fettuccine
¹/₂ cup refrigerated pesto sauce
1 tablespoon lemon juice
1 cup shredded fresh spinach

1 small red onion, thinly sliced
¹/₂ cup coarsely chopped seeded tomato
2 tablespoons pine nuts or slivered
    almonds, toasted

1

Cook pasta according to package directions. Drain. Rinse with cold water; drain again.

2

In a large bowl combine pesto sauce and lemon juice. Add pasta. Toss to coat.

3

Add spinach, red onion, and tomato to the pasta mixture; toss until mixed. Sprinkle with nuts.

Nutrition Facts per serving: 224 calories, 15 g total fat, 2 mg cholesterol, 150 mg sodium, 19 g carbohydrate, 6 g protein.

RUFFLED PASTA WITH WILTED GREENS

Toss the hot pasta mixture with the salad greens just until the greens start to wilt. Serve the salad warm.

Start to Finish: 25 minutes **Makes:** 6 servings

2 cups dried pasta ruffles or
    corkscrew macaroni (rotini)
    (about 6 ounces)
2 tablespoons water
2 tablespoons dry sherry
2 tablespoons soy sauce
1 tablespoon lemon juice

1 tablespoon honey
1 large red onion, thinly sliced and
    separated into rings
1 tablespoon sesame seeds
2 tablespoons sesame oil or cooking
    oil
6 cups torn mixed salad greens

1

Cook pasta according to package directions. Drain. Rinse with cold water; drain again.

2

Meanwhile, in a small bowl combine the water, sherry, soy sauce, lemon juice, and honey. Set aside.

3

In a large skillet cook onion and sesame seeds in hot oil about 5 minutes or until onion is tender and seeds are toasted. Stir in soy mixture. Bring to boiling; remove from heat. Add pasta; toss until coated.

4

Place greens in a large salad bowl. Pour pasta mixture over greens. Toss just until greens start to wilt. Serve immediately.

Nutrition Facts per serving: 188 calories, 6 g total fat, 0 mg cholesterol, 350 mg sodium, 28 g carbohydrate, 5 g protein.

MEXICAN-STYLE SPAGHETTI

Salsa and fresh cilantro contribute the south-of-the-border flavor.

Start to Finish: 25 minutes **Makes:** 4 servings

4 ounces dried spaghetti or linguine, broken

1 8³/₄-ounce can whole kernel corn, drained

³/₄ cup bottled chunky salsa

¹/₄ cup pitted ripe olives, sliced

1 tablespoon snipped fresh cilantro (optional)

¹/₄ cup shredded Colby and Monterey Jack cheese (optional)

Fresh cilantro sprig (optional)

1
Cook pasta according to package directions. Drain. Return to pan.

2
Add corn, salsa, olives, and, if desired, snipped cilantro. Toss over low heat until pasta is coated and mixture is hot. If desired, sprinkle with cheese. If desired, garnish with cilantro sprig.

Nutrition Facts per serving: 171 calories, 3 g total fat, 0 mg cholesterol, 339 mg sodium, 34 g carbohydrate, 6 g protein.

GARLIC ASPARAGUS AND PASTA WITH LEMON CREAM

Whipping cream and a generous amount of lemon peel make an elegant sauce for pasta with vegetables. (Pictured on page 213.)

Start to Finish: 25 minutes **Makes:** 4 servings

8 ounces dried mafalda or corkscrew macaroni (rotini)

2 cups fresh asparagus cut into 2-inch pieces

8 baby sunburst squash and/or pattypan squash,* halved (4 ounces)

2 cloves garlic, minced

1 tablespoon margarine or butter

1/2 cup whipping cream

2 teaspoons finely shredded lemon peel

Paprika (optional)

1

Cook pasta according to package directions. Drain. Cover and keep warm.

2

Meanwhile, in a large skillet cook asparagus, squash, and garlic in hot margarine or butter for 2 to 3 minutes or until vegetables are crisp-tender, stirring frequently. Remove with a slotted spoon and add to pasta.

3

Add whipping cream and lemon peel to skillet; bring to boiling. Boil for 2 to 3 minutes or until reduced to 1/3 cup. To serve, pour cream mixture over pasta mixture. Toss gently to coat. If desired, sprinkle with paprika.

Nutrition Facts per serving: 370 calories, 15 g total fat, 41 mg cholesterol, 49 mg sodium, 49 g carbohydrate, 10 g protein.

*Note: One medium zucchini or yellow summer squash cut into 8 pieces may be substituted for the baby sunburst squash and/or pattypan squash.

FRESH VEGETABLE PASTA SALAD

This recipe gives three cheese options, but you can branch out even farther and use cheddar, Monterey Jack, or any other firm cheese.

Start to Finish: 25 minutes **Makes:** 6 servings

¼ cup loosely packed fresh parsley sprigs

2 tablespoons salad oil

2 tablespoons wine vinegar

2 tablespoons water

1 to 2 cloves garlic

½ teaspoon dry mustard

¼ teaspoon salt

¼ teaspoon ground black pepper

2 ounces dried linguine or fettuccine, broken

1 large carrot, cut into thin strips

1 small turnip, cut into thin strips

1 small zucchini, cut into thin strips

½ cup chopped red sweet pepper

½ cup frozen peas, thawed

½ cup cubed part-skim mozzarella, Gruyère, or Swiss cheese (2 ounces)

1

For dressing, in a blender container combine parsley sprigs, oil, wine vinegar, the water, garlic, dry mustard, salt, and black pepper. Cover and blend until combined. Set aside.

2

Cook pasta according to package directions, adding carrot and turnip for the last 4 minutes of cooking. Drain pasta and vegetables. Rinse with cold water; drain again.

3

In a large salad bowl combine the cooked pasta and vegetables, the zucchini, sweet pepper, peas, and cheese. Add the dressing. Toss lightly to coat.

Nutrition Facts per serving: 155 calories, 7 g total fat, 27 mg cholesterol, 166 mg sodium, 18 g carbohydrate, 6 g protein.

MUSHROOM TORTELLONI IN CURRY CREAM

Serve this tantalizing soup with broiled chicken, steamed broccoli, and fresh fruit.

Start to Finish: 30 minutes **Makes:** 5 servings

1 shallot, finely chopped
1 fresh jalapeño pepper,* seeded and
   finely chopped
1 clove garlic, minced
2 teaspoons curry powder
1 tablespoon cooking oil
1 14-ounce can chicken broth

1 14-ounce can unsweetened coconut
   milk
1 9-ounce package refrigerated
   mushroom-filled tortelloni or
   cheese-filled tortellini
1 tablespoon snipped fresh basil
1 medium tomato, chopped
   Chopped peanuts (optional)

1

In a medium saucepan cook shallot, jalapeño pepper, garlic, and curry powder in hot oil about
1 minute or until shallot is tender. Stir in chicken broth. Bring to boiling; reduce heat. Cover and
simmer for 5 minutes.

2

Stir in the coconut milk, pasta, and basil. Cook and stir about 5 minutes more or until pasta is tender
but still firm. Stir in the tomato. Cook and stir until heated through; do not boil. If desired, garnish
each serving with peanuts.

Nutrition Facts per serving: 343 calories, 21 g total fat, 19 mg cholesterol, 509 mg sodium, 29 g carbohydrate, 10 g protein.

*Note: Because chile peppers, such as jalapeños, contain volatile oils that can burn your skin and
eyes, avoid direct contact with them as much as possible. When working with chile peppers, wear
plastic or rubber gloves. If your bare hands do touch the chile peppers, wash your hands and nails well
with soap and warm water.

ANGEL HAIR PASTA WITH CREAMY MUSHROOM SAUCE

Cream cheese is the base for the rich and creamy sauce.

Start to Finish: 20 minutes **Makes:** 4 servings

4 ounces dried angel hair pasta (capellini) or spaghettini (thin spaghetti)

$1\frac{1}{2}$ cups sliced fresh mushrooms

1 medium onion, chopped

1 tablespoon margarine or butter

1 3-ounce package cream cheese, cut into cubes

$\frac{1}{4}$ teaspoon salt

$\frac{1}{8}$ teaspoon ground black pepper

$\frac{1}{3}$ cup milk

2 tablespoons snipped fresh chives

1

Cook pasta according to package directions. Drain. Cover and keep warm.

2

Meanwhile, for sauce, in a medium saucepan cook the mushrooms and onion in the hot margarine or butter until vegetables are tender. Stir in cream cheese, salt, and pepper. Cook and stir over low heat until cream cheese melts. Gradually stir in milk and chives; heat through.

3

Pour sauce over pasta. Toss to coat.

Nutrition Facts per serving: 234 calories, 11 g total fat, 25 mg cholesterol, 243 mg sodium, 27 g carbohydrate, 7 g protein.

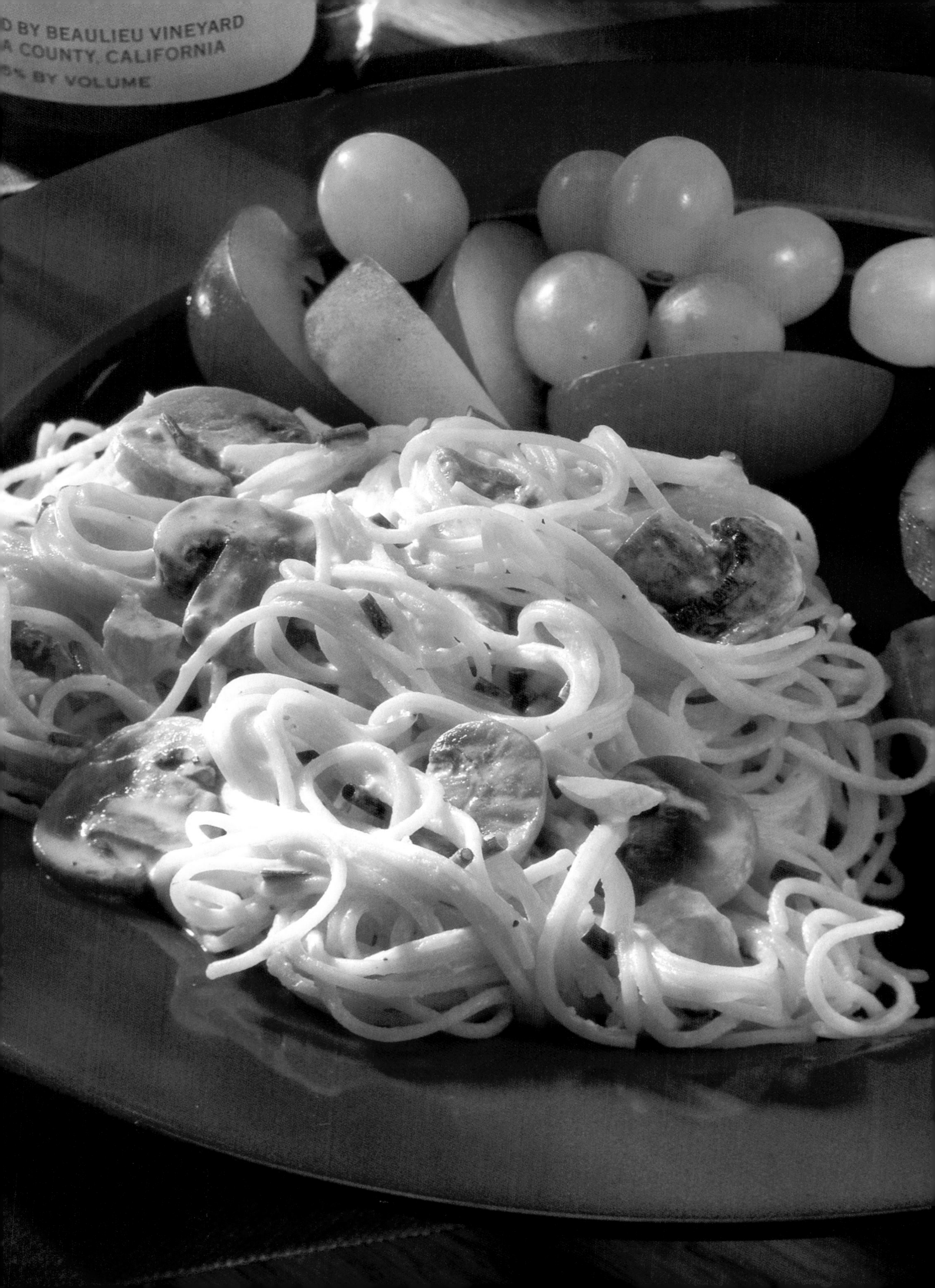
D BY BEAULIEU VINEYARD
A COUNTY, CALIFORNIA
% BY VOLUME

FARFALLE WITH SPINACH AND MUSHROOMS

Whether you call it farfalle or bow ties, the pasta shaped like butterflies will intrigue your dinner guests.

Start to Finish: 30 minutes **Makes:** 4 or 5 servings

3 cups dried large bow ties (farfalle) or 2 cups dried medium shell macaroni (6 ounces)

1 medium onion, chopped

1 cup sliced fresh portobellos or other fresh mushrooms (such as chanterelles, shiitake, and/or crimini)

2 cloves garlic, minced

1 tablespoon margarine or butter

4 cups thinly sliced fresh spinach

1 teaspoon snipped fresh thyme

$\frac{1}{8}$ teaspoon ground black pepper

1 tablespoon licorice-flavored liqueur (optional)

2 tablespoons shredded Parmesan cheese

1

Cook pasta according to package directions. Drain. Cover and keep warm.

2

Meanwhile, in a large skillet cook onion, mushrooms, and garlic in hot margarine or butter for 2 to 3 minutes or until mushrooms are nearly tender. Stir in spinach, thyme, and pepper; cook 1 minute more or until heated through and spinach is slightly wilted. Stir in cooked pasta and, if desired, liqueur. Toss gently to mix. Sprinkle with Parmesan cheese.

Nutrition Facts per serving: 214 calories, 6 g total fat, 39 mg cholesterol, 127 mg sodium, 33 g carbohydrate, 9 g protein.

LINGUINE WITH CREAMY SPINACH PESTO

Serve this cheesy pasta side dish with broiled or grilled steaks, burgers, or chops.

Start to Finish: 20 minutes **Makes:** 8 servings

8 ounces dried linguine or fettuccine
½ cup firmly packed fresh spinach
⅓ cup semisoft cheese with spiced garlic and herbs
¼ cup grated Parmesan cheese (1 ounce)
3 tablespoons pine nuts, toasted

2 tablespoons snipped fresh basil or 2 teaspoons dried basil, crushed
2 tablespoons olive oil or cooking oil
¼ teaspoon salt
1 clove garlic, minced
Fresh basil sprigs (optional)
Sliced radishes (optional)

1

Cook pasta according to package directions. Drain. Cover and keep warm.

2

Meanwhile, in a blender container or food processor bowl combine spinach, semisoft cheese, Parmesan cheese, pine nuts, snipped or dried basil, oil, salt, and garlic. Cover and blend or process until smooth.

3

Place pasta in a warm serving bowl. Add spinach mixture. Toss gently to coat. If desired, garnish with basil sprigs and radishes.

Nutrition Facts per serving: 216 calories, 11 g total fat, 14 mg cholesterol, 161 mg sodium, 24 g carbohydrate, 7 g protein.

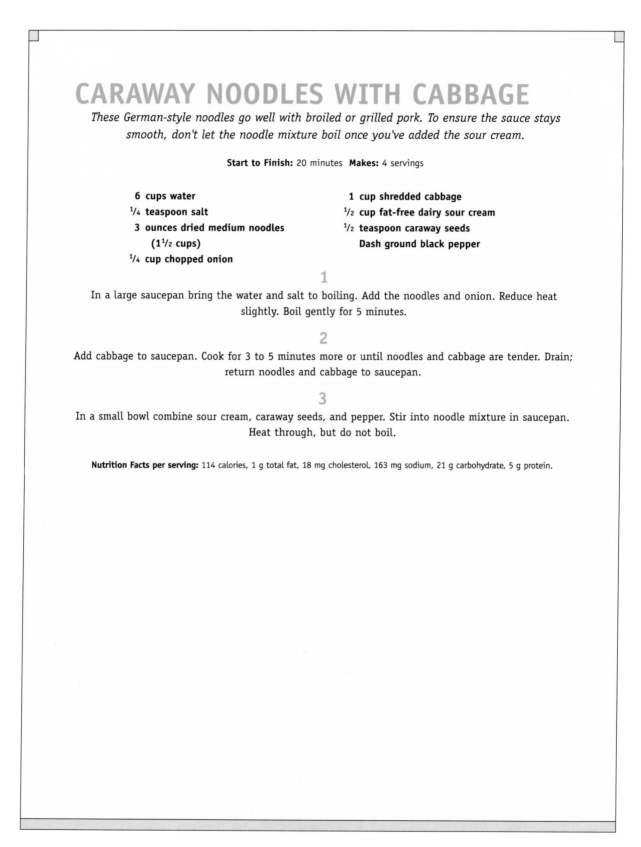

CARAWAY NOODLES WITH CABBAGE

These German-style noodles go well with broiled or grilled pork. To ensure the sauce stays smooth, don't let the noodle mixture boil once you've added the sour cream.

Start to Finish: 20 minutes **Makes:** 4 servings

6 cups water	1 cup shredded cabbage
¼ teaspoon salt	½ cup fat-free dairy sour cream
3 ounces dried medium noodles (1½ cups)	½ teaspoon caraway seeds
¼ cup chopped onion	Dash ground black pepper

1

In a large saucepan bring the water and salt to boiling. Add the noodles and onion. Reduce heat slightly. Boil gently for 5 minutes.

2

Add cabbage to saucepan. Cook for 3 to 5 minutes more or until noodles and cabbage are tender. Drain; return noodles and cabbage to saucepan.

3

In a small bowl combine sour cream, caraway seeds, and pepper. Stir into noodle mixture in saucepan. Heat through, but do not boil.

Nutrition Facts per serving: 114 calories, 1 g total fat, 18 mg cholesterol, 163 mg sodium, 21 g carbohydrate, 5 g protein.

PASTA WITH BROCCOLI-ONION SAUCE

Another time, try this pasta with cauliflower florets or sliced carrots.

Start to Finish: 25 minutes **Makes:** 5 servings

3 ounces packaged dried linguine or
  fettuccine
1½ cups broccoli florets
  Nonstick cooking spray
1 medium onion, thinly sliced and
  separated into rings
¾ cup fat-free milk
2 teaspoons cornstarch

1 teaspoon instant chicken bouillon
  granules
  Dash ground black pepper
  Dash ground nutmeg
½ cup shredded part-skim mozzarella
  cheese (2 ounces)
1 tablespoon dry white wine
  (optional)

1

Cook pasta according to the package directions, adding the broccoli for the last 5 minutes of cooking.
Drain; return pasta and broccoli to saucepan. Cover and keep warm.

2

Meanwhile, coat an unheated large skillet with nonstick cooking spray. Preheat over medium-low heat.
Add onion. Cover and cook for 8 to 10 minutes or until onion is tender, stirring occasionally.

3

In a small bowl stir together the milk, cornstarch, bouillon granules, pepper, and nutmeg. Add to onion
in skillet. Cook and stir over medium heat until thickened and bubbly. Cook and stir for 2 minutes
more. Stir in cheese and, if desired, wine until cheese is melted. Pour cheese mixture over cooked pasta
and broccoli; toss to coat.

Nutrition Facts per serving: 138 calories, 2 g total fat, 7 mg cholesterol, 285 mg sodium, 20 g carbohydrate, 8 g protein.

PENNE WITH BROCCOLI AND DRIED TOMATOES

Shiitake mushrooms lend an Asian touch to this otherwise Mediterranean-style side dish.

Start to Finish: 25 minutes **Makes:** 4 servings

8 ounces dried tomato-basil or regular penne (mostaccoli) or regular ziti (2¼ cups)

4 cups broccoli florets

½ cup oil-packed dried tomatoes

1 cup sliced fresh shiitake mushrooms

¼ teaspoon crushed red pepper

3 cloves garlic, minced

½ cup snipped fresh basil

1

Cook pasta according to package directions, adding broccoli for the last 2 minutes of cooking. Drain; return pasta and broccoli to saucepan. Cover and keep warm.

2

Meanwhile, drain tomatoes, reserving 2 tablespoons of the oil. Cut tomatoes into strips.

3

In a medium saucepan cook mushrooms, crushed red pepper, and garlic in reserved oil for 3 to 4 minutes or until mushrooms are tender. Stir in basil. Add to pasta along with tomato strips; toss gently to combine.

Nutrition Facts per serving: 348 calories, 10 g total fat, 0 mg cholesterol, 70 mg sodium, 55 g carbohydrate, 12 g protein.

LINGUINE WITH MIXED NUTS AND GORGONZOLA

Toasting the nuts in a mixture of butter and olive oil adds extra nuttiness and richness.

Start to Finish: 15 minutes **Makes:** 6 or 7 servings

1 9-ounce package refrigerated linguine or fettuccine

$^3/_4$ cup chopped hazelnuts (filberts), pecans, and/or pine nuts

1 tablespoon butter

1 tablespoon olive oil

$^1/_2$ cup crumbled Gorgonzola or other blue cheese (2 ounces)

$^1/_4$ cup shredded Parmesan cheese (1 ounce)

2 tablespoons snipped fresh basil

Fresh basil leaves (optional)

1

Cook pasta according to package directions. Drain. Cover and keep warm.

2

Meanwhile, in a medium skillet cook the hazelnuts, pecans, or pine nuts in hot butter and olive oil until toasted and butter begins to brown, stirring frequently. Add nut mixture to pasta. Add the Gorgonzola or other blue cheese, Parmesan cheese, and the snipped basil. Toss gently to coat. If desired, garnish with basil leaves.

Nutrition Facts per serving: 298 calories, 19 g total fat, 23 mg cholesterol, 212 mg sodium, 25 g carbohydrate, 9 g protein.

MIXED PASTAS WITH FRESH HERBS

Enhance the appearance of this five-ingredient side dish by using a variety of pasta shapes.
Choose shapes that cook in about the same amount of time.

Start to Finish: 20 minutes **Makes:** 8 servings

8 ounces assorted dried pastas*
2 tablespoons walnut oil or olive oil
2 tablespoons snipped assorted fresh
  herbs (such as sage, rosemary, and
  basil)

¼ teaspoon salt
¼ teaspoon coarsely ground black
  pepper
  Assorted fresh herb leaves
  (optional)

1

Cook pasta according to package directions. Drain. Toss the hot pasta with the oil, snipped herbs, salt,
and pepper. If desired, garnish with herb leaves.

Nutrition Facts per serving: 170 calories, 7 g total fat, 0 mg cholesterol, 67 mg sodium, 22 g carbohydrate, 4 g protein.

*Note: Trenne and red pepper quadrelle are shown in the photo.

LEMON-BASIL PASTA WITH VEGETABLES

You'll find a wide variety of loose-pack frozen vegetable combinations at the supermarket. Use whichever one you like.

Start to Finish: 25 minutes **Makes:** 4 servings

1 cup dried orecchiette, medium shell macaroni, or corkscrew macaroni (rotini) (about 3 ounces)

$1^1/_2$ cups loose-pack frozen broccoli, French-style green beans, pearl onions, and red sweet pepper or other frozen vegetable combination

3 tablespoons margarine or butter

1 tablespoon snipped fresh parsley

1 clove garlic, minced

1 teaspoon finely shredded lemon peel

$^1/_2$ teaspoon dried basil, crushed

$^1/_8$ teaspoon salt

Dash ground red pepper

1

Cook pasta according to package directions, adding the frozen vegetables for the last 5 minutes of cooking. Drain. Cover and keep warm.

2

Meanwhile, in a small saucepan melt the margarine or butter. Stir in parsley, garlic, lemon peel, basil, salt, and ground red pepper. Pour over pasta mixture. Toss to coat.

Nutrition Facts per serving: 178 calories, 9 g total fat, 0 mg cholesterol, 176 mg sodium, 20 g carbohydrate, 4 g protein.

ORZO WITH
MUSHROOMS AND LEEKS

If you have garlic cloves on hand, mince 1 clove and substitute it for the bottled minced garlic.

Start to Finish: 25 minutes **Makes:** 4 to 6 servings

³/₄ cup dried orzo (rosamarina)

4 ounces assorted fresh mushrooms
(such as porcini, crimini,
chanterelle, shiitake, and button),
sliced or quartered (1¹/₂ cups)

1 leek or 2 large green onions,
chopped (about ¹/₃ cup)

¹/₂ teaspoon bottled minced garlic

¹/₄ teaspoon ground black pepper

¹/₈ teaspoon salt

1 tablespoon margarine or butter

¹/₄ cup water

¹/₂ to 1 teaspoon snipped fresh
marjoram or ¹/₄ teaspoon dried
marjoram, crushed

¹/₂ teaspoon instant beef or chicken
bouillon granules

Grated Romano cheese (optional)

Fresh marjoram sprigs (optional)

1

Cook pasta according to package directions. Drain. Cover and keep warm.

2

Meanwhile, in a large skillet cook mushrooms, leek or green onions, garlic, pepper, and salt in hot margarine or butter over medium-high heat for 5 minutes. Add the water, snipped or dried marjoram, and bouillon granules. Reduce heat; cook about 6 minutes or until liquid is almost absorbed. Toss the mushroom mixture with the pasta. If desired, sprinkle with Romano cheese. If desired, garnish with marjoram sprigs.

Nutrition Facts per serving: 167 calories, 4 g total fat, 8 mg cholesterol, 209 mg sodium, 29 g carbohydrate, 5 g protein.

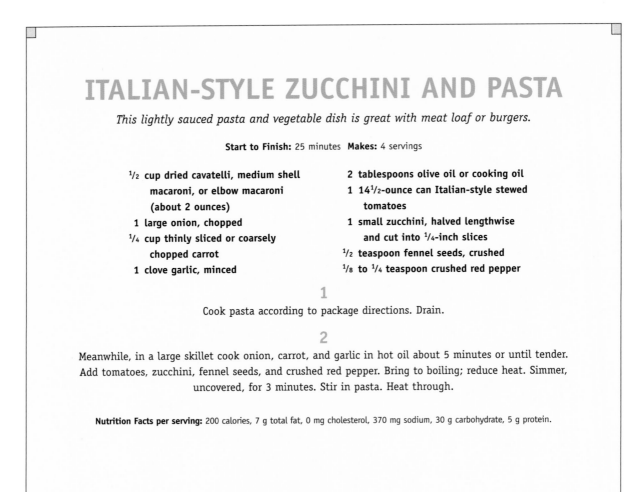

ITALIAN-STYLE ZUCCHINI AND PASTA

This lightly sauced pasta and vegetable dish is great with meat loaf or burgers.

Start to Finish: 25 minutes   **Makes:** 4 servings

¹/₂ cup dried cavatelli, medium shell
   macaroni, or elbow macaroni
   (about 2 ounces)
1 large onion, chopped
¹/₄ cup thinly sliced or coarsely
   chopped carrot
1 clove garlic, minced

2 tablespoons olive oil or cooking oil
1 14¹/₂-ounce can Italian-style stewed
   tomatoes
1 small zucchini, halved lengthwise
   and cut into ¹/₄-inch slices
¹/₂ teaspoon fennel seeds, crushed
¹/₈ to ¹/₄ teaspoon crushed red pepper

1

Cook pasta according to package directions. Drain.

2

Meanwhile, in a large skillet cook onion, carrot, and garlic in hot oil about 5 minutes or until tender.
Add tomatoes, zucchini, fennel seeds, and crushed red pepper. Bring to boiling; reduce heat. Simmer,
uncovered, for 3 minutes. Stir in pasta. Heat through.

Nutrition Facts per serving: 200 calories, 7 g total fat, 0 mg cholesterol, 370 mg sodium, 30 g carbohydrate, 5 g protein.

PEPPER-OLIVE PASTA SALAD

The more the merrier is certainly true for this zesty salad. The more pasta shapes, that is. Mix several shapes (of similar size) to make 3 cups uncooked pasta.

Start to Finish: 25 minutes **Makes:** 8 to 10 servings

3 cups dried small pasta (such as penne [mostaccioli], radiatore, corkscrew macaroni [rotini], and/or wagon wheel macaroni [ruote]) (about 9 ounces)

¼ cup olive oil

2 tablespoons balsamic vinegar or wine vinegar

½ teaspoon finely shredded lemon peel

2 tablespoons lemon juice

1 to 2 tablespoons sugar (optional)

1 tablespoon Dijon-style mustard

1 teaspoon snipped fresh basil or ¼ to ½ teaspoon dried basil, crushed

1 teaspoon snipped fresh thyme or ¼ to ½ teaspoon dried thyme, crushed

½ teaspoon snipped fresh marjoram or ¼ to ½ teaspoon dried marjoram, crushed

¼ teaspoon ground black pepper

2 yellow, red, and/or green sweet peppers, cut into thin bite-size strips

½ cup pitted green olives, drained and halved

½ cup thinly sliced green onions

1

Cook pasta according to package directions. Drain. Rinse with cold water; drain again.

2

For dressing, in a screw-top jar combine olive oil, balsamic or wine vinegar, lemon peel, lemon juice, sugar (if desired), mustard, basil, thyme, marjoram, and black pepper. Cover and shake well.

3

In a large salad bowl combine the pasta sweet pepper strips, olives, and green onions.
Add dressing. Toss gently to coat.

Nutrition Facts per serving: 193 calories, 8 g total fat, 0 mg cholesterol, 211 mg sodium, 26 g carbohydrate, 4 g protein.

WILD-ABOUT-MUSHROOMS PASTA

If you prefer to use dried rather than fresh mushrooms, use 1 cup assorted dried mushrooms. Soak the dried mushrooms in boiling water for 30 minutes. Drain and thinly slice the mushrooms. Then, cook the mushrooms as directed in the recipe.

Start to Finish: 25 minutes **Makes:** 4 servings

3 ounces dried mafalda, pappardelle, or medium shell macaroni
2 tablespoons butter or margarine
1 tablespoon olive oil
8 ounces assorted fresh mushrooms (such as oyster, shiitake, chanterelle, and button), thinly sliced

1/4 teaspoon cracked black pepper
1/8 teaspoon salt
1 to 2 teaspoons snipped fresh herbs (such as thyme, oregano, basil, or rosemary) (optional)

1

Cook pasta according to package directions. Drain. Cover and keep warm.

2

Meanwhile, in a large skillet heat butter or margarine and oil over medium heat. Add mushrooms, pepper, and salt; cook, uncovered, about 8 minutes or until tender, stirring occasionally. Remove from heat. If desired, stir in herbs. Let stand for 3 minutes. Add pasta. Toss to coat.

Nutrition Facts per serving: 147 calories, 6 g total fat, 15 mg cholesterol, 126 mg sodium, 19 g carbohydrate, 4 g protein.

ZITI WITH BLUE CHEESE SAUCE

For a little extra tang, sprinkle additional blue cheese over the pasta mixture just before serving.

Start to Finish: 25 minutes **Makes:** 6 servings

1 cup dried cut ziti or corkscrew
  macaroni (rotini) (about
  3 ounces)
3 cups loose-pack frozen broccoli,
  cauliflower, and carrots
2 tablespoons margarine or butter
2 tablespoons all-purpose flour

$\frac{1}{8}$ teaspoon salt
$\frac{1}{8}$ teaspoon ground black pepper
1 cup milk
$\frac{1}{2}$ cup crumbled blue cheese
  (2 ounces)
$\frac{1}{3}$ cup dairy sour cream
Crumbled blue cheese (optional)

1

Cook pasta according to package directions, adding frozen vegetables for the last 7 minutes of cooking. Drain pasta and vegetables.

2

Meanwhile, for sauce, in a small saucepan melt margarine or butter. Stir in flour, salt, and pepper. Add milk all at once. Cook and stir until thickened and bubbly. Cook and stir for 1 minute more. Remove from heat. Stir in the $\frac{1}{2}$ cup blue cheese and the sour cream.

3

Pour sauce over pasta mixture. Toss to coat. If desired, sprinkle with additional blue cheese.

Nutrition Facts per serving: 223 calories, 10 g total fat, 16 mg cholesterol, 280 mg sodium, 26 g carbohydrate, 8 g protein.

INDEX

A-B

Alfredo, Broccoli and Chicken
  Fettuccine, 90
Alfredo with Roasted Peppers,
  Tortellini, 114
Angel Hair Pasta with Chicken and
  Shrimp, 48
Angel Hair Pasta with Creamy
  Mushroom Sauce, 224
Artichokes
  Fettuccine with Artichokes and
    Basil, 64
  Pasta with Tuna, Roasted
    Peppers, and Artichokes, 166
  Three-Cheese Orzo Salad, 210
  Tortellini with Creamy
    Vegetables, 118
Asian Chicken Noodle Soup, 146
Asparagus
  Bow Ties with Asparagus, 176
  Garlic Asparagus and Pasta with
    Lemon Cream, 220
  Pasta with Ricotta and
    Vegetables, 172
  Rotini and Sweet Pepper
    Primavera, 112
  Spring Green Pasta Soup, 158
  Tortellini-Caesar Salad, 204
Bail-Out Beef Stroganoff, 12
Baked Cavatelli, 125
Baked Ravioli with Meat Sauce, 124
Beans (*see also* **Green Beans**)
  Chicken-Vegetable Ratatouille, 92
  Chili-Sauced Pasta, 110
  Fish and Shell Stew, 156
  Ham, Pasta, and Bean Soup, 144
  Mexican Fiesta Salad, 194
  Penne with Fennel, 68
  South-of-the-Border Bean and
    Pasta Salad, 198
  Turkey-Mac Chili, 94
  White Bean and Sausage
    Rigatoni, 96
Beef (*see also* **Beef, Ground**)
  Bail-Out Beef Stroganoff, 12
  Beef-Vegetable Stew with
    Pasta, 142
  Southwest Beef-Linguine Toss, 18
  Stir-Fried Beef and Ramen
    Noodles, 20
Beef, Ground
  Baked Ravioli with Meat Sauce, 124
  Chili Macaroni, 14
  Greek-Style Pasta Skillet, 36

Beef, Ground (*continued*)
  Mediterranean Mostaccioli, 28
  Saucy Spiced Shells, 122
Bow Ties and Cheese, 138
Bow Ties with Asparagus, 176
Bow Ties with Sausage and Sweet
  Peppers, 22
Bow Ties with Scallops and Chard
  Sauce, 58
Broccoli
  Bail-Out Beef Stroganoff, 12
  Broccoli and Chicken Fettuccine
    Alfredo, 90
  Chicken and Pasta Toss, 38
  Deli-Style Pasta Salad, 208
  Fettuccine with Creamy Ham
    Sauce, 83
  Herbed Turkey and Broccoli, 168
  Lemon-Basil Pasta with
    Vegetables, 238
  Lemony Scallops and
    Spaghettini, 104
  Pasta with Broccoli-Onion
    Sauce, 231
  Pasta with Ricotta and
    Vegetables, 172
  Penne with Broccoli and Dried
    Tomatoes, 232
  Salmon-Pasta Salad, 192
  Teriyaki Penne, 76
  Turkey-and-Broccoli-Filled Lasagna
    Rolls, 132
  Tuscan Ravioli Stew, 152
  Ziti with Blue Cheese Sauce, 248

C

Cabbage
  Caraway Noodles with Cabbage, 230
  Penne Salad with Italian Beans
    and Gorgonzola, 180
  Shanghai Pork Lo Mein, 30
  Soba Noodles with Spring
    Vegetables, 86
Caraway Noodles with Cabbage, 230
Carrots
  Asian Chicken Noodle Soup, 146
  Baked Ravioli with Meat Sauce, 124
  Chicken and Pasta Toss, 38
  Chicken-Vegetable Ratatouille, 92
  Creamy Carrot and Pasta Soup, 160
  Deli-Style Pasta Salad, 208
  Fresh Vegetable Pasta Salad, 221
  Hot and Sour Soup, 157

Carrots (*continued*)
  Italian-Style Zucchini and Pasta, 242
  Soba Noodles with Spring
    Vegetables, 86
  Soup with Mixed Pastas, 150
  Stir-Fried Beef and Ramen
    Noodles, 20
  Summer Squash Primavera, 66
  Teriyaki Chicken Noodle
    Salad, 184
  Trattoria-Style Spinach
    Fettuccine, 74
  Ziti with Blue Cheese Sauce, 248
Cheese
  Angel Hair Pasta with Creamy
    Mushroom Sauce, 224
  Baked Cavatelli, 125
  Baked Ravioli with Meat Sauce, 124
  Bow Ties and Cheese, 138
  Chicken and Penne with Basil
    Sauce, 44
  Chicken and Prosciutto Pasta, 128
  Chili Macaroni, 14
  Creamy Three-Cheese and Toasted
    Walnut Pasta, 178
  Farfalle with Spinach and
    Mushrooms, 226
  Fettuccine alla Carbonara, 116
  Fettuccine and Salmon, 98
  Fettuccine Straw and Hay with
    Parmesan, 26
  Fettuccine with Creamy Ham
    Sauce, 83
  Fettuccine with Herbed Shrimp, 102
  Fontina and Melon Salad, 202
  Fresh Pasta with Sun-Dried Tomato
    Pesto, 170
  Fresh Vegetable Pasta
    Salad, 221
  Greek-Style Pasta Skillet, 36
  Grilled Vegetable Salad with
    Garlic Dressing, 200
  Herbed Shrimp-Pasta Medley, 62
  Herbed Turkey and Broccoli, 168
  Italian Croutons, 204
  Linguine with Creamy Spinach
    Pesto, 228
  Linguine with Mixed Nuts and
    Gorgonzola, 234
  Mexican Fiesta Salad, 194
  New Millennium Macaroni and
    Cheese, 136
  Pasta-Fruit Salad, 206
  Pasta Rosa Verde, 72
  Pasta with Basil Cream Sauce, 82
  Pasta with Broccoli-Onion Sauce, 231

Cheese *(continued)*
Pasta with Chèvre, 173
Pasta with Pesto-Tomato Sauce, 174
Pasta with Ricotta and
Vegetables, 172
Pasta with Smoked Salmon and
Lemon Cream, 101
Pasta with Spinach and Smoked
Sausage, 52
Penne Salad with Italian Beans
and Gorgonzola, 180
Penne with Fennel, 68
Salmon-Pasta Salad, 192
South-of-the-Border Bean and
Pasta Salad, 198
Southwestern Pasta, 70
Spicy Pasta Pie, 130
Spinach and Orzo Pie, 134
Spinach Lasagna, 139
Summer Squash Primavera, 66
Three-Cheese Orzo Salad, 210
Tortellini-Caesar Salad, 204
Tortellini with Creamy
Vegetables, 118
Trattoria-Style Spinach
Fettuccine, 74
Turkey-and-Broccoli-Filled Lasagna
Rolls, 132
Tuscan Ravioli Stew, 152
White Bean and Sausage
Rigatoni, 96
Ziti with Blue Cheese Sauce, 248
Chicken
Angel Hair Pasta with Chicken
and Shrimp, 48
Asian Chicken Noodle Soup, 146
Broccoli and Chicken Fettuccine
Alfredo, 90
Chicken-and-Melon-Stuffed
Shells, 187
Chicken and Pasta Toss, 38
Chicken and Penne with Basil
Sauce, 44
Chicken and Prosciutto Pasta, 128
Chicken Noodle Soup Florentine, 148
Chicken-Vegetable Ratatouille, 92
Crab and Pasta Gazpacho, 154
Fettuccine with Sweet Peppers
and Onions, 46
Fruited Chicken-Pasta Salad, 186
Lemon-Pepper Pasta and Chicken, 40
Pasta with Spinach and Smoked
Sausage, 52
Soba Noodles with Spring
Vegetables, 86
Soup with Mixed Pastas, 150
Stroganoff-Style Chicken, 50
Summer Chicken and Mushroom
Pasta, 42
Teriyaki Chicken Noodle Salad, 184
Tortellini with Tomato, Chicken,
and Basil Sauce, 88
Turkey-and-Broccoli-Filled Lasagna
Rolls, 132
Turkey-Mac Chili, 94

Chili Macaroni, 14
Chili-Sauced Pasta, 110
Chili, Turkey-Mac, 94
Clam Sauce, Ravioli with Red, 106
Corn
Jalapeño Corn Chowder, 162
Mexican Fiesta Salad, 194
Mexican-Style Spaghetti, 218
Southwest Beef-Linguine Toss, 18
Crab
Crab and Pasta Gazpacho, 154
Hot and Sour Soup, 157
Creamy Carrot and Pasta Soup, 160
Creamy Three-Cheese and Toasted
Walnut Pasta, 178
Croutons, Italian, 204

D-G

Deli-Style Pasta Salad, 208
Easy Salmon Pasta, 100
Eggplant
Chicken-Vegetable Ratatouille, 92
Grilled Vegetable Salad with
Garlic Dressing, 200
Mediterranean Mostaccioli, 28
Farfalle with Spinach and
Mushrooms, 226
Fettuccine alla Carbonara, 116
Fettuccine and Salmon, 98
Fettuccine Straw and Hay with
Parmesan, 26
Fettuccine with Artichokes and
Basil, 64
Fettuccine with Creamy Ham
Sauce, 83
Fettuccine with Herbed Shrimp, 102
Fettuccine with Sweet Peppers and
Onions, 46
Fish
Easy Salmon Pasta, 100
Fettuccine and Salmon, 98
Fish and Shell Stew, 156
Pasta with Smoked Salmon and
Lemon Cream, 101
Pasta with Tuna, Roasted
Peppers, and Artichokes, 166
Salmon-Pasta Salad, 192
Saucy Fish Fillets with Pasta, 54
Florentine Pasta Salad, 214
Fontina and Melon Salad, 202
Fresh Herbs
Angel Hair Pasta with Creamy
Mushroom Sauce, 224
Bail-Out Beef Stroganoff, 12
Bow Ties with Asparagus, 176
Bow Ties with Sausage and
Sweet Peppers, 22
Chicken-and-Melon-Stuffed
Shells, 187

Fresh Herbs *(continued)*
Chicken and Penne with Basil
Sauce, 44
Crab and Pasta Gazpacho, 154
Farfalle with Spinach and
Mushrooms, 226
Fettuccine alla Carbonara, 116
Fettuccine and Salmon, 98
Fettuccine with Artichokes and
Basil, 64
Fettuccine with Herbed Shrimp, 102
Fettuccine with Sweet Peppers
and Onions, 46
Fresh Vegetable Pasta Salad, 221
Grilled Vegetable Salad with
Garlic Dressing, 200
Ham and Vegetables with Penne, 84
Herbed Shrimp-Pasta Medley, 62
Lemon-Basil Pasta with
Vegetables, 238
Lemon-Pepper Pasta and Chicken, 40
Linguine with Creamy Spinach
Pesto, 228
Linguine with Mixed Nuts and
Gorgonzola, 234
Mediterranean Mostaccioli, 28
Mexican Fiesta Salad, 194
Mixed Pastas with Fresh Herbs, 236
Mushroom Tortelloni in Curry
Cream, 222
Orzo with Mushrooms and Leeks, 240
Pasta with Basil Cream Sauce, 82
Pasta with Chèvre, 173
Pasta with Pepperoni Marinara, 24
Pasta with Pesto-Tomato Sauce, 174
Pasta with Ricotta and
Vegetables, 172
Pasta with Smoked Salmon and
Lemon Cream, 101
Pasta with Spinach and Smoked
Sausage, 52
Pasta with Tuna, Roasted
Peppers, and Artichokes, 166
Penne Salad with Italian Beans
and Gorgonzola, 180
Penne with Broccoli and Dried
Tomatoes, 232
Penne with Rustic Tomatoes, 56
Pepper-Olive Pasta Salad, 244
Roasted Red Pepper Sauce over
Tortellini, 80
Rotini and Sweet Pepper
Primavera, 112
Salmon-Pasta Salad, 192
Shrimp and Tomatoes with Pasta, 60
Soup with Mixed Pastas, 150
Southwestern Pasta, 70
Spaetzle with Caramelized
Onions, 32
Spring Green Pasta Soup, 158
Stir-Fried Beef and Ramen
Noodles, 20
Summer Chicken and Mushroom
Pasta, 42

Fresh Herbs *(continued)*
Summer Squash Primavera, 66
Three-Cheese Orzo Salad, 210
Tomatoes and Ravioli with
Escarole, 16
Tortellini Alfredo with Roasted
Peppers, 114
Tortellini-Vegetable Salad, 196
Tortellini with Tomato, Chicken,
and Basil Sauce, 88
Turkey-and-Broccoli-Filled Lasagna
Rolls, 132
Turkey and Pasta Salad, 188
Tuscan Ravioli Stew, 152
White Bean and Sausage
Rigatoni, 96
Wild-About-Mushrooms Pasta, 246
Fresh Pasta with Sun-Dried Tomato
Pesto, 170
Fresh Vegetable Pasta Salad, 221
Fruits
Chicken-and-Melon-Stuffed
Shells, 187
Crab and Pasta Gazpacho, 154
Fontina and Melon Salad, 202
Fruited Chicken-Pasta Salad, 186
Pasta-Fruit Salad, 206
Turkey and Pasta Salad, 188
Garlic
Angel Hair Pasta with Chicken and
Shrimp, 48
Baked Cavatelli, 125
Beef-Vegetable Stew with Pasta, 142
Bow Ties with Scallops and Chard
Sauce, 58
Chicken and Penne with Basil
Sauce, 44
Chicken and Prosciutto Pasta, 128
Chicken-Vegetable Ratatouille, 92
Farfalle with Spinach and
Mushrooms, 226
Fettuccine with Artichokes and
Basil, 64
Fettuccine with Herbed Shrimp, 102
Fettuccine with Sweet Peppers
and Onions, 46
Fresh Pasta with Sun-Dried Tomato
Pesto, 170
Garlic Asparagus and Pasta with
Lemon Cream, 220
Ham, Spinach, and Mostaccioli
Casserole, 126
Herbed Shrimp-Pasta Medley, 62
Lemon-Pepper Pasta and Chicken, 40
New Millennium Macaroni and
Cheese, 136
Pasta Rosa Verde, 72
Pasta with Pesto-Tomato Sauce, 174
Pasta with Spinach and Smoked
Sausage, 52
Pasta with Tuna, Roasted Peppers,
and Artichokes, 166

Garlic *(continued)*
Penne with Broccoli and Dried
Tomatoes, 232
Penne with Fennel, 68
Penne with Rustic Tomatoes, 56
Roasted Garlic Dressing, 200
Roasted Red Pepper Sauce over
Tortellini, 80
Shrimp and Tomatoes with Pasta, 60
Soup with Mixed Pastas, 150
Southwestern Pasta, 70
Spinach Lasagna, 139
Spring Green Pasta Soup, 158
Summer Chicken and Mushroom
Pasta, 42
Summer Squash Primavera, 66
Tomatoes and Ravioli with Escarole, 16
Tortellini-Vegetable Salad, 196
Turkey-Mac Chili, 94
Tuscan Ravioli Stew, 152
Wilted Greens with Dried Tomatoes
and Pasta, 171
Greek-Style Pasta Skillet, 36
Green Beans
Chicken-Vegetable Ratatouille, 92
Chili Macaroni, 14
Greek-Style Pasta Skillet, 36
Lemon-Basil Pasta with
Vegetables, 238
Pasta with Ricotta and
Vegetables, 172
Penne Salad with Italian Beans
and Gorgonzola, 180
Summer Pasta with Pork, 34
Greens
Bow Ties with Scallops and Chard
Sauce, 58
Chicken Noodle Soup Florentine, 148
Farfalle with Spinach and
Mushrooms, 226
Florentine Pasta Salad, 214
Fontina and Melon Salad, 202
Herbed Shrimp-Pasta Medley, 62
Linguine with Creamy Spinach
Pesto, 228
Pasta Rosa Verde, 72
Pasta with Spinach and Smoked
Sausage, 52
Penne Salad with Italian Beans
and Gorgonzola, 180
Ruffled Pasta with Wilted
Greens, 216
South-of-the-Border Bean and
Pasta Salad, 198
Teriyaki Chicken Noodle Salad, 184
Tomatoes and Ravioli with
Escarole, 16
Tortellini-Caesar Salad, 204
Tortellini-Vegetable Salad, 196
Wilted Greens with Dried Tomatoes
and Pasta, 171
Grilled Vegetable Salad with Garlic
Dressing, 200

H-L

Ham
Baked Ravioli with Meat Sauce, 124
Chicken and Prosciutto Pasta, 128
Fettuccine with Creamy Ham
Sauce, 83
Ham and Chutney Pasta Salad, 190
Ham and Vegetables with Penne, 84
Ham, Pasta, and Bean Soup, 144
Ham, Spinach, and Mostaccioli
Casserole, 126
Spaetzle with Caramelized
Onions, 32
Herbed Shrimp-Pasta Medley, 62
Herbed Turkey and Broccoli, 168
Hoisin-Glazed Turkey Medallions, 51
Hot and Sour Soup, 157
Italian Croutons, 204
Italian-Style Zucchini and Pasta, 242
Jalapeño Corn Chowder, 162
Lamb
Greek-Style Pasta Skillet, 36
Mediterranean Mostaccioli, 28
Saucy Spiced Shells, 122
Lemons
Bow Ties with Asparagus, 176
Lemon-Basil Pasta with
Vegetables, 238
Lemon-Pepper Pasta and Chicken, 40
Lemony Scallops and
Spaghettini, 104
Pasta with Smoked Salmon and
Lemon Cream, 101
Linguine with Creamy Spinach
Pesto, 228
Linguine with Fennel and Shrimp
in Orange Sauce, 108
Linguine with Mixed Nuts and
Gorgonzola, 234

M-O

Meatless Entrées
Bow Ties and Cheese, 138
Bow Ties with Asparagus, 176
Chili-Sauced Pasta, 110
Creamy Carrot and Pasta Soup, 160
Creamy Three-Cheese and Toasted
Walnut Pasta, 178
Deli-Style Pasta Salad, 208
Fettuccine with Artichokes and
Basil, 64
Fontina and Melon Salad, 202
Fresh Pasta with Sun-Dried Tomato
Pesto, 170
Grilled Vegetable Salad with
Garlic Dressing, 200
Jalapeño Corn Chowder, 162
Mexican Fiesta Salad, 194
New Millennium Macaroni and
Cheese, 136

Meatless Entrées *(continued)*
Pasta-Fruit Salad, 206
Pasta Rosa Verde, 72
Pasta with Chèvre, 173
Pasta with Pesto-Tomato Sauce, 174
Pasta with Ricotta and
    Vegetables, 172
Penne Salad with Italian Beans
    and Gorgonzola, 180
Penne with Broccoli and Dried
    Tomatoes, 232
Penne with Fennel, 68
Rotini and Sweet Pepper
    Primavera, 112
South-of-the-Border Bean and
    Pasta Salad, 198
Southwestern Pasta, 70
Spinach and Orzo Pie, 134
Spinach Lasagna, 139
Spring Green Pasta Soup, 158
Summer Squash Primavera, 66
Teriyaki Penne, 76
Three-Cheese Orzo Salad, 210
Tortellini-Vegetable Salad, 196
Tortellini with Creamy
    Vegetables, 118
Trattoria-Style Spinach
    Fettuccine, 74
Wilted Greens with Dried Tomatoes
    and Pasta, 171
Mediterranean Mostaccioli, 28
Mexican Fiesta Salad, 194
Mexican-Style Spaghetti, 218
Mixed Pastas with Fresh Herbs, 236
Mushrooms
Angel Hair Pasta with Creamy
    Mushroom Sauce, 224
Beef-Vegetable Stew with Pasta, 142
Chicken Noodle Soup Florentine, 148
Farfalle with Spinach and
    Mushrooms, 226
Fettuccine with Creamy Ham
    Sauce, 83
Fettuccine with Herbed Shrimp, 102
Hot and Sour Soup, 157
Mushroom Tortelloni in Curry
    Cream, 222
Orzo with Mushrooms and
    Leeks, 240
Penne with Broccoli and Dried
    Tomatoes, 232
Spicy Pasta Pie, 130
Spinach Lasagna, 139
Stroganoff-Style Chicken, 50
Summer Chicken and Mushroom
    Pasta, 42
Summer Pasta with Pork, 34
Teriyaki Penne, 76
Tomatoes and Ravioli with
    Escarole, 16
Tortellini-Vegetable Salad, 196
Wild-About-Mushrooms Pasta, 246
New Millennium Macaroni and
    Cheese, 136

Nuts
Creamy Three-Cheese and Toasted
    Walnut Pasta, 178
Florentine Pasta Salad, 214
Fresh Pasta with Sun-Dried Tomato
    Pesto, 170
Hoisin-Glazed Turkey Medallions, 51
Linguine with Creamy Spinach
    Pesto, 228
Linguine with Mixed Nuts and
    Gorgonzola, 234
Pasta-Fruit Salad, 206
Pasta Rosa Verde, 72
Pasta with Pesto-Tomato Sauce, 174
Summer Squash Primavera, 66
Tomatoes and Ravioli with
    Escarole, 16
Onions, Spaetzle with Caramelized, 32
Oranges
Fruited Chicken-Pasta Salad, 186
Linguine with Fennel and Shrimp
    in Orange Sauce, 108
Pasta-Fruit Salad, 206
Shanghai Pork Lo Mein, 30
Teriyaki Chicken Noodle Salad, 184
Orzo with Mushrooms and Leeks, 240

P-R

Pasta-Fruit Salad, 206
Pasta Rosa Verde, 72
Pasta with Basil Cream Sauce, 82
Pasta with Broccoli-Onion Sauce, 231
Pasta with Chèvre, 173
Pasta with Pepperoni Marinara, 24
Pasta with Pesto-Tomato Sauce, 174
Pasta with Ricotta and
    Vegetables, 172
Pasta with Smoked Salmon and Lemon
    Cream, 101
Pasta with Spinach and Smoked
    Sausage, 52
Pasta with Tuna, Roasted Peppers,
    and Artichokes, 166
Pea Pods
Asian Chicken Noodle Soup, 146
Soba Noodles with Spring
    Vegetables, 86
Stir-Fried Beef and Ramen
    Noodles, 20
Teriyaki Chicken Noodle Salad, 184
Tortellini with Creamy
    Vegetables, 118
Peas
Beef-Vegetable Stew with Pasta, 142
Bow Ties with Asparagus, 176
Creamy Three-Cheese and Toasted
    Walnut Pasta, 178
Fettuccine Straw and Hay with
    Parmesan, 26
Fresh Vegetable Pasta Salad, 221
Lemon-Pepper Pasta and Chicken, 40

Peas *(continued)*
Pasta with Basil Cream Sauce, 82
Spring Green Pasta Soup, 158
Three-Cheese Orzo Salad, 210
Penne Salad with Italian Beans and
    Gorgonzola, 180
Penne with Broccoli and Dried
    Tomatoes, 232
Penne with Fennel, 68
Penne with Rustic Tomatoes, 56
Peppers, Chile
Chili Macaroni, 14
Jalapeño Corn Chowder, 162
Mushroom Tortelloni in Curry
    Cream, 222
South-of-the-Border Bean and
    Pasta Salad, 198
Southwestern Pasta, 70
Peppers, Sweet
Angel Hair Pasta with Chicken
    and Shrimp, 48
Asian Chicken Noodle Soup, 146
Bow Ties with Sausage and
    Sweet Peppers, 22
Chicken and Penne with Basil
    Sauce, 44
Chicken and Prosciutto Pasta, 128
Chili-Sauced Pasta, 110
Deli-Style Pasta Salad, 208
Fettuccine with Artichokes and
    Basil, 64
Fettuccine with Sweet Peppers
    and Onions, 46
Fresh Vegetable Pasta Salad, 221
Grilled Vegetable Salad with
    Garlic Dressing, 200
Jalapeño Corn Chowder, 162
Lemon-Basil Pasta with
    Vegetables, 238
New Millennium Macaroni and
    Cheese, 136
Pasta with Chèvre, 173
Pasta with Spinach and Smoked
    Sausage, 52
Pasta with Tuna, Roasted
    Peppers, and Artichokes, 166
Penne with Fennel, 68
Pepper-Olive Pasta Salad, 244
Roasted Red Pepper Sauce over
    Tortellini, 80
Rotini and Sweet Pepper
    Primavera, 112
Saucy Spiced Shells, 122
Southwest Beef-Linguine Toss, 18
Spaetzle with Caramelized
    Onions, 32
Spinach Lasagna, 139
Summer Squash Primavera, 66
Tortellini Alfredo with Roasted
    Peppers, 114
Tortellini-Vegetable Salad, 196
Tortellini with Creamy
    Vegetables, 118

Pork
Baked Ravioli with Meat Sauce, 124
Bow Ties with Sausage and
Sweet Peppers, 22
Fettuccine alla Carbonara, 116
Fettuccine Straw and Hay with
Parmesan, 26
Pasta with Basil Cream Sauce, 82
Pasta with Pepperoni Marinara, 24
Saucy Spiced Shells, 122
Shanghai Pork Lo Mein, 30
Spaetzle with Caramelized
Onions, 32
Summer Pasta with Pork, 34
Ravioli with Red Clam Sauce, 106
Roasted Garlic Dressing, 200
Roasted Red Pepper Sauce over
Tortellini, 80
Rotini and Sweet Pepper
Primavera, 112
Ruffled Pasta with Wilted Greens, 216

S

Salad Dressings
Roasted Garlic Dressing, 200
Salsa Dressing, 198
Salad, Main-Dish *(see also pages 182-211)*
Salads, Side-Dish
Florentine Pasta Salad, 214
Fresh Vegetable Pasta Salad, 221
Penne Salad with Italian Beans
and Gorgonzola, 180
Pepper-Olive Pasta Salad, 244
Ruffled Pasta with Wilted
Greens, 216
Salmon
Easy Salmon Pasta, 100
Fettuccine and Salmon, 98
Pasta with Smoked Salmon and
Lemon Cream, 101
Salmon-Pasta Salad, 192
Salsa Dressing, 198
Saucy Fish Fillets with Pasta, 54
Saucy Spiced Shells, 122
Sausage
Baked Cavatelli, 125
Baked Ravioli with Meat Sauce, 124
Bow Ties with Sausage and
Sweet Peppers, 22
Pasta with Pepperoni Marinara, 24
Pasta with Spinach and Smoked
Sausage, 52
Spicy Pasta Pie, 130
White Bean and Sausage
Rigatoni, 96

Scallops
Bow Ties with Scallops and Chard
Sauce, 58
Lemony Scallops and
Spaghettini, 104
Shanghai Pork Lo Mein, 30
Shrimp
Angel Hair Pasta with Chicken
and Shrimp, 48
Fettuccine with Herbed Shrimp, 102
Herbed Shrimp-Pasta Medley, 62
Linguine with Fennel and Shrimp
in Orange Sauce, 108
Shrimp and Tomatoes with
Pasta, 60
Soba Noodles with Spring
Vegetables, 86
Soup with Mixed Pastas, 150
South-of-the-Border Bean and
Pasta Salad, 198
Southwest Beef-Linguine Toss, 18
Southwestern Pasta, 70
Spaetzle with Caramelized Onions, 32
Spicy Pasta Pie, 130
Spinach and Orzo Pie, 134
Spinach Lasagna, 139
Spring Green Pasta Soup, 158
Stir-Fries
Angel Hair Pasta with Chicken
and Shrimp, 48
Chicken and Pasta Toss, 38
Chicken and Penne with Basil
Sauce, 44
Shanghai Pork Lo Mein, 30
Southwest Beef-Linguine Toss, 18
Stir-Fried Beef and Ramen
Noodles, 20
Stroganoff, Bail-Out Beef, 12
Stroganoff-Style Chicken, 50
Sugar Snap Peas
Beef-Vegetable Stew with
Pasta, 142
Spring Green Pasta Soup, 158
Three-Cheese Orzo Salad, 210
Summer Chicken and Mushroom
Pasta, 42
Summer Pasta with Pork, 34
Summer Squash Primavera, 66

T-Z

Teriyaki Chicken Noodle Salad, 184
Teriyaki Penne, 76
Three-Cheese Orzo Salad, 210
Tomatoes and Ravioli with Escarole, 16
Tortellini Alfredo with Roasted
Peppers, 114
Tortellini-Caesar Salad, 204
Tortellini-Vegetable Salad, 196

Tortellini with Creamy Vegetables, 118
Tortellini with Tomato, Chicken,
and Basil Sauce, 88
Trattoria-Style Spinach Fettuccine, 74
Tuna, Roasted Peppers, and
Artichokes, Pasta with, 166
Turkey
Asian Chicken Noodle Soup, 146
Broccoli and Chicken Fettuccine
Alfredo, 90
Chili Macaroni, 14
Fruited Chicken-Pasta Salad, 186
Ham, Pasta, and Bean Soup, 144
Herbed Turkey and Broccoli, 168
Hoisin-Glazed Turkey Medallions, 51
Pasta with Spinach and Smoked
Sausage, 52
Soba Noodles with Spring
Vegetables, 86
Spicy Pasta Pie, 130
Turkey-and-Broccoli-Filled Lasagna
Rolls, 132
Turkey and Pasta Salad, 188
Turkey-Mac Chili, 94
White Bean and Sausage
Rigatoni, 96
Tuscan Ravioli Stew, 152
White Bean and Sausage Rigatoni, 96
Wilted Greens with Dried Tomatoes and
Pasta, 171
Wild-About-Mushrooms Pasta, 246
Ziti with Blue Cheese Sauce, 248
Zucchini and Other Summer Squash
Angel Hair Pasta with Chicken
and Shrimp, 48
Chicken-Vegetable Ratatouille, 92
Fresh Vegetable Pasta Salad, 221
Garlic Asparagus and Pasta with
Lemon Cream, 220
Grilled Vegetable Salad with
Garlic Dressing, 200
Ham and Vegetables with Penne, 84
Herbed Shrimp-Pasta Medley, 62
Italian-Style Zucchini and
Pasta, 242
Mediterranean Mostaccioli, 28
Mexican Fiesta Salad, 194
Pasta with Smoked Salmon and
Lemon Cream, 101
Ravioli with Red Clam Sauce, 106
Rotini and Sweet Pepper
Primavera, 112
Summer Pasta with Pork, 34
Summer Squash Primavera, 66
Teriyaki Chicken Noodle Salad, 184

Emergency Substitutions

It you don't have:	Substitute:
Bacon, 1 slice, crisp-cooked, crumbled	1 tablespoon cooked bacon pieces
Baking powder, 1 teaspoon	½ teaspoon cream of tartar plus ¼ teaspoon baking soda
Balsamic vinegar, 1 tablespoon	1 tablespoon cider vinegar or red wine vinegar plus ½ teaspoon sugar
Bread crumbs, fine dry, ¼ cup	¾ cup soft bread crumbs, or ¼ cup cracker crumbs, or ¼ cup cornflake crumbs
Broth, beef or chicken, 1 cup	1 teaspoon or 1 cube instant beef or chicken bouillon plus 1 cup hot water
Butter, 1 cup	1 cup shortening plus ¼ teaspoon salt, if desired
Buttermilk, 1 cup	1 tablespoon lemon juice or vinegar plus enough milk to make 1 cup (let stand 5 minutes before using) or 1 cup plain yogurt
Chocolate, semisweet, 1 ounce	3 tablespoons semisweet chocolate pieces, or 1 ounce unsweetened chocolate plus 1 tablespoon granulated sugar, or 1 tablespoon unsweetened cocoa powder plus 2 teaspoons sugar and 2 teaspoons shortening
Chocolate, sweet baking, 4 ounces	¼ cup unsweetened cocoa powder plus ⅓ cup granulated sugar and 3 tablespoons shortening
Chocolate, unsweetened, 1 ounce	3 tablespoons unsweetened cocoa powder plus 1 tablespoon cooking oil or shortening, melted
Cornstarch, 1 tablespoon (for thickening)	2 tablespoons all-purpose flour
Corn syrup (light), 1 cup	1 cup granulated sugar plus ¼ cup water
Egg, 1 whole	2 egg whites, or 2 egg yolks, or ¼ cup refrigerated or frozen egg product, thawed
Flour, cake, 1 cup	1 cup minus 2 tablespoons all-purpose flour
Flour, self-rising, 1 cup	1 cup all-purpose flour plus 1 teaspoon baking powder, ½ teaspoon salt, and ¼ teaspoon baking soda
Garlic, 1 clove	½ teaspoon bottled minced garlic or ⅛ teaspoon garlic powder
Ginger, grated fresh, 1 teaspoon	¼ teaspoon ground ginger
Half-and-half or light cream, 1 cup	1 tablespoon melted butter or margarine plus enough whole milk to make 1 cup
Molasses, 1 cup	1 cup honey
Mustard, dry, 1 teaspoon	1 tablespoon prepared (in cooked mixtures)
Mustard, prepared, 1 tablespoon	½ teaspoon dry mustard plus 2 teaspoons vinegar
Onion, chopped, ½ cup	2 tablespoons dried minced onion or ½ teaspoon onion powder
Sour cream, dairy, 1 cup	1 cup plain yogurt
Sugar, granulated, 1 cup	1 cup packed brown sugar or 2 cups sifted powdered sugar
Sugar, brown, 1 cup packed	1 cup granulated sugar plus 2 tablespoons molasses
Tomato juice, 1 cup	½ cup tomato sauce plus ½ cup water
Tomato sauce, 2 cups	¾ cup tomato paste plus 1 cup water
Vanilla bean, 1 whole	2 teaspoons vanilla extract
Wine, red, 1 cup	1 cup beef or chicken broth in savory recipes; cranberry juice in desserts
Wine, white, 1 cup	1 cup chicken broth in savory recipes; apple juice or white grape juice in desserts
Yeast, active dry, 1 package	about 2¼ teaspoons active dry yeast

Seasonings

Apple pie spice, 1 teaspoon	½ teaspoon ground cinnamon plus ¼ teaspoon ground nutmeg, ⅛ teaspoon ground allspice, and dash ground cloves or ginger
Cajun seasoning, 1 tablespoon	½ teaspoon white pepper, ½ teaspoon garlic powder, ½ teaspoon onion powder, ½ teaspoon ground red pepper, ½ teaspoon paprika, and ½ teaspoon ground black pepper
Herbs, snipped fresh, 1 tablespoon	½ to 1 teaspoon dried herb, crushed, or ½ teaspoon ground herb
Poultry seasoning, 1 teaspoon	¾ teaspoon dried sage, crushed, plus ¼ teaspoon dried thyme or marjoram, crushed
Pumpkin pie spice, 1 teaspoon	½ teaspoon ground cinnamon plus ¼ teaspoon ground ginger, ¼ teaspoon ground allspice, and ⅛ teaspoon ground nutmeg

Metric Information

The charts on this page provide a guide for converting measurements from the U.S. customary system, which is used throughout this book, to the metric system.

Product Differences

Most of the ingredients called for in the recipes in this book are available in most countries. However, some are known by different names. Here are some common American ingredients and their possible counterparts:

- Sugar (white) is granulated, fine granulated, or castor sugar.
- Powdered sugar is icing sugar.
- All-purpose flour is enriched, bleached or unbleached, white household flour. When self-rising flour is used in place of all-purpose flour in a recipe that calls for leavening, omit the leavening agent (baking soda or baking powder) and salt.
- Light-colored corn syrup is golden syrup.
- Cornstarch is cornflour.
- Baking soda is bicarbonate of soda.
- Vanilla or vanilla extract is vanilla essence.
- Green, red, or yellow sweet peppers are capsicums or bell peppers.
- Golden raisins are sultanas.

Volume and Weight

The United States traditionally uses cup measures for liquid and solid ingredients. The chart below shows the approximate imperial and metric equivalents. If you are accustomed to weighing solid ingredients, the following approximate equivalents will be helpful.

- 1 cup butter, castor sugar, or rice = 8 ounces = ½ pound = 250 grams
- 1 cup flour = 4 ounces = ¼ pound = 125 grams
- 1 cup icing sugar = 5 ounces = 150 grams

Canadian and U.S. volume for a cup measure is 8 fluid ounces (237 ml), but the standard metric equivalent is 250 ml.

1 British imperial cup is 10 fluid ounces.

In Australia, 1 tablespoon equals 20 ml, and there are 4 teaspoons in the Australian tablespoon.

Spoon measures are used for smaller amounts of ingredients Although the size of the tablespoon varies slightly in different countries, for practical purposes and for recipes in this book a straight substitution is all that's necessary. Measurements made using cups or spoons always should be level unless stated otherwise.

Common Weight Range Replacements

Imperial / U.S.	Metric
½ ounce	15 g
1 ounce	25 g or 30 g
4 ounces (¼ pound)	115 g or 125 g
8 ounces (½ pound)	225 g or 250 g
16 ounces (1 pound)	450 g or 500 g
1¼ pounds	625 g
1½ pounds	750 g
2 pounds or 2¼ pounds	1,000 g or 1 Kg

Oven Temperature Equivalents

Fahrenheit Setting	Celsius Setting*	Gas Setting
300°F	150°C	Gas Mark 2 (very low)
325°F	160°C	Gas Mark 3 (low)
350°F	180°C	Gas Mark 4 (moderate)
375°F	190°C	Gas Mark 5 (moderate)
400°F	200°C	Gas Mark 6 (hot)
425°F	220°C	Gas Mark 7 (hot)
450°F	230°C	Gas Mark 8 (very hot)
475°F	240°C	Gas Mark 9 (very hot)
500°F	260°C	Gas Mark 10 (extremely hot)
Broil	Broil	Grill

*Electric and gas ovens may be calibrated using celsius. However, for an electric oven, increase celsius setting 10 to 20 degrees when cooking above 160°C. For convection or forced air ovens (gas or electric), lower the temperature setting 25°F/10°C when cooking at all heat levels.

Baking Pan Sizes

Imperial / U.S.	Metric
9×1½-inch round cake pan	22- or 23×4-cm (1.5 L)
9×1½-inch pie plate	22- or 23×4-cm (1 L)
8×8×2-inch square cake pan	20×5-cm (2 L)
9×9×2-inch square cake pan	22- or 23×4.5-cm (2.5 L)
11×7×1½-inch baking pan	28×17×4-cm (2 L)
2-quart rectangular baking pan	30×19×4.5-cm (3 L)
13×9×2-inch baking pan	34×22×4.5-cm (3.5 L)
15×10×1-inch jelly roll pan	40×25×2-cm
9×5×3-inch loaf pan	23×13×8-cm (2 L)
2-quart casserole	2 L

U.S. / Standard Metric Equivalents

⅛ teaspoon = 0.5 ml

¼ teaspoon = 1 ml

½ teaspoon = 2 ml

1 teaspoon = 5 ml

1 tablespoon = 15 ml

2 tablespoons = 25 ml

¼ cup = 2 fluid ounces = 50 ml

⅓ cup = 3 fluid ounces = 75 ml

½ cup = 4 fluid ounces = 125 ml

⅔ cup = 5 fluid ounces = 150 ml

¾ cup = 6 fluid ounces = 175 ml

1 cup = 8 fluid ounces = 250 ml

2 cups = 1 pint = 500 ml

1 quart = 1 litre